Texas Ranger
Johnny Klevenhagen

Douglas V. Meed

Republic of Texas Press
Plano, Texas

Library of Congress Cataloging-in-Publication Data

Meed, Douglas V.
  Texas Ranger : Johnny Klevenhagen / Douglas V. Meed.
      p. cm.
  Includes bibliographical references (p.) and index.
  ISBN 1-55622-793-0 (pbk.)
  1. Klevenhagen, Johnny, 1912-1958   2. Texas Rangers—Biography.   I. Title.
  HV7911.K58 M44 2000
  363.2'092—dc21   00-035300
  [B]   CIP

© 2000, Douglas V. Meed

Republic of Texas Press is an imprint of Wordware Publishing, Inc.
No part of this book may be reproduced in any form or by
any means without permission in writing from
Wordware Publishing, Inc.

Printed in the United States of America

ISBN 1-55622-793-0
10 9 8 7 6 5 4 3 2 1
0004

All inquiries for volume purchases of this book should be addressed to
Wordware Publishing, Inc., at 2320 Los Rios Boulevard, Plano, Texas
75074. Telephone inquiries may be made by calling:

(972) 423-0090

Contents

Introduction vii

Chapter 1   Early Days 1

Chapter 2   The Red River Raider 11

Chapter 3   The Bridegroom Bank Bandit 25

Chapter 4   Alligator Joe. 35

Chapter 5   With the Rangers 51

Chapter 6   The Beaumont Riots. 61

Chapter 7   The Late Giacona 69

Chapter 8   The Brute's Last Mistake 75

Chapter 9   Murder, Gangland Style. 81

Chapter 10   Carlino on Trial 93

Chapter 11   Such a Nice Young Man 107

Chapter 12   Of Jail Breaks and Barbers 119

Chapter 13   The Chicago Chums 127

Chapter 14   Three Punks and a Gorgeous Carhop . . . 135

Chapter 15   Dukes of Duval. 147

Chapter 16   Cop Killer 161

Chapter 17   Norris—The Smiling Killer. 173

Chapter 18   Alton's Demons 187

Chapter 19   The Free State of Galveston 199

Chapter 20   Trail's End 209

Chapter 21   L'envoi 223

Bibliography 229

Index 237

For Alex

*****

Acknowledgments

This book could not have been written without the generous help of the Klevenhagen family, John J. Jr., John J. III, Viola, and Carolyn.

Also, my heartfelt thanks for their help and encouragement to: My wife, Jeannine; Robert Stonedale, Palacios; Louis and Barbara Dartez, Houston; Terry McCollister, El Paso; Janice Rogers (nee Lewis), College Station; Retired Texas Ranger Edgar D. Gooding; Burleson County Sheriff Gene Barber; Paulett Srubar, Somerville Chamber of Commerce; and former sheriff of Brazoria County Robert Gladney.

Many thanks go to the librarians at the Center for American History, University of Texas, Austin; the Texas State Library, Austin; the Houston Metropolitan Research Center, Houston Public Library; the Rosenberg Library, Galveston; the Texas Ranger Hall of Fame and Museum, Ft. Fisher, Waco; and the San Antonio Texas Ranger Museum.

Texas Ranger Captain John J. Klevenhagen Sr. is considered to have
been one of the most outstanding leaders of an elite corps of law officers.
(Photo courtesy of Houston Public Library)

Introduction

For more than a century and a half the Texas Rangers have dedicated themselves to the protection of life and property in that vast empire known as Texas. Their methods have changed over the years. Now, they are more inclined to use aircraft rather than horses and utilize DNA and fingerprint evidence from a laboratory rather than following spoor through the brush.

But if the tactics of criminology have changed, the men have not. They are still fearless, tough, taciturn, and often very compassionate men.

Johnny Klevenhagen was the paradigm of that type of unchanging Ranger. He was tall, lean, and leathery with blue-gray eyes that could sparkle with humor and sometimes mist with sympathy. To lawbreakers, however, his eyes were like x-rays that could burn through lies and evasions and lay bare a criminal's hidden deeds.

Johnny bridged the gap between the old and the new ways of the Rangers, holding fast to the best traditions while eagerly grasping the new and scientific. During the time he was a nemesis to Texas lawbreakers, the state underwent one of its most dramatic changes.

During the 1930s Texas was rural. Agriculture, ranching, and the growing petroleum industry were the mainstays of the economy. And on the farms, ranches, and in the small towns where the bulk of the population lived, many Texans had not journeyed fifty miles from their birthplace.

But by the end of the 1950s, the state had undergone a massive transformation. World War II and rapid industrialization had turned the state into a land of big cities with exploding populations. Petrochemical complexes, steel mills, shipyards, aircraft plants, and a myriad of other manufacturing facilities as well as the always-booming construction industry changed the face of the land.

And Texans too grew into a more sophisticated, well-educated, and traveled people as perhaps the greatest growth came in the schools and particularly the colleges and universities, whose boom was fueled by growing demands for more educated and skilled citizens.

Johnny also grew with Texas. From a rural lad on a Comal County ranch, by study and hard work, he became one of the premier lawmen in an organization that was already legendary.

As a lawman he was relentless and unstoppable as in the famous dictum of Ranger Captain Bill MacDonald: "No man in the wrong can stand up to a man in the right who keeps on coming." Johnny Klevenhagen always kept on coming. He devoted his life to the people of Texas. It wore him out and eventually killed him, but he left a legacy of dedication and heroism that will never be forgotten by those men who uniquely bear the title of Texas Rangers.

CHAPTER 1

Early Days

The life of the cowboy in the hardscrabble mesquite and brush country of Comal County, Texas, was not a job for the fainthearted. It was a land that bred lean, tough, and determined people who could fight perennial drought, occasional floods, flaying summer heat, and the chilling "northers" that screamed down in winter.

There were rattlesnakes in the brush that would lash out and poison unwary cattle, coyotes that would feast on a newborn calf, diseases that could wipe out a herd in a week. And during the first and second decades of this century there were still rustlers who would strip a rancher of the stock he had labored to raise and protect. This was the hard country into which Johnny Klevenhagen was born.

He was the son of a Comal County rancher named Frank Klevenhagen. His mother, the former Mary Videau, gave birth to the famed lawman on June 2, 1912, at the family ranch house near New Braunfels. The county seat, New Braunfels, was a thriving farming town of 6,000. In fact, there were only 8,000 people in all of Comal County, and they were greatly outnumbered by the cattle and, according to a few cynics, by the horde of rattlesnakes that infested the mesquite and cedar brakes.

In the harsh ranch environment Johnny learned to do chores, ride and rope, and shoot only a few years after he learned to walk. He grew up wearing the high-heeled, needle-toed cowboy boots and became so accustomed to them he found it difficult to walk in regular shoes. "They make me feel as if I'm falling over backwards," he once said. His first heroes were his dad and older brother George. But when rustlers struck their ranch and other neighboring spreads and the Texas Rangers were called to the area, he found additional heroes and a lifelong calling.

The Rangers were big men with high boots, big sombreros, wearing a distinctive badge fashioned from a Mexican silver peso. They carried their saddles in the trunks of their automobiles and their "thumbbuster" Colt six-shooters slung on belt holsters or stuck in their trousers to lay across their bellies. They walked with the slight swagger of men who feared little and knew much.

From his first glimpse of these swashbucklers, Johnny knew his life would belong to the Texas Rangers. The glamour of the Rangers, however, seemed remote from the wearying chores of a small ranch, although it lifted his spirits when a party of Rangers camped nearby.

On those happy occasions Johnny would ride to their campsite where he was always welcomed by the big men. He sat by the evening fires, swallowed their black coffee and thrilled to their talk about how to follow trail sign; wild tales about "popping caps," Ranger slang for shootouts; and stories of long hours on stakeouts where they lived on cigarettes, black coffee, and adrenaline.

But being a peace officer had to wait. Johnny was too young and his dad needed his help on the ranch so he dropped out of school during the eighth grade to work full time. To bring in more cash, when he was sixteen years old he moved to San Antonio where he was hired as a lineman for the San Antonio Electric Company.

After a year on that job, he still burned with ambition to become a police officer, and in 1930, after his seventeenth birthday, he figured a way to join the San Antonio Police Department. First he grew and cultivated, as best he could, a rather luxuriant black mustache. The next step was proof of age.

At that time, in order to vote, Texans were required to be twenty-one years of age and to purchase a poll tax, which cost one dollar. If during the Depression of the 1930s many did not have a dollar to spare, why then a willing politician would buy one for you. Reciprocity was, of course, expected. Somehow, Johnny managed to wrangle a poll tax receipt with his name on it.

With the document, at six-feet-two-inches in height, looming even larger in cowboy boots, and with his premature leathery look thanks to hours in the saddle under a blistering Texas sun, he was able to convince the authorities he was of age. He was hired as a motorcycle policeman by the San Antonio Police Department. "I was only seventeen," he later said, "I guess I fudged a little."

His first move was to buy an old "thumbbuster" .45-caliber, single-action Colt revolver. He later told crime writer Stan Redding, "I took to those motorcycles like a duck to water. Hell, it wasn't much different than riding a raw horse."

Nineteen thirty was a busy year for police officers. The failure of the stock market and the ensuing Depression engulfed the country in growing poverty, and that combined with the general lawlessness that came with Prohibition, made police work more hazardous than during the days of the old frontier. There was growing unem-

Young Klevenhagen started his career in law
enforcement as a San Antonio Police motorcycle
officer in 1930.

ployment in the cities, and the collapse of agricultural
prices bankrupted many farmers, leading to foreclosures of
homesteads held by some families for one hundred years.

Many proud men became desperate and embittered.
Fast automobiles, confused police jurisdictions, and the

lack of police professionalism made the decade of the 1930s the heyday of the bank robber and the bootlegger and marked the beginnings of organized crime. The headlines belonged to Pretty Boy Floyd, Bonnie and Clyde, Baby Face Nelson, and John Dillinger, all of whom were lionized in the popular press as the Robin Hoods and the James Boys of the day.

To police officers, however, they were the same vicious criminals with whom they had always warred. It was in this environment that Johnny began his life's work.

With a population of 200,000, San Antonio in the 1930s was a city of great beauty with the San Antonio River flowing lazily through the center of downtown, brightly colored flowers blossoming from the wide front yards of stately homes, and ancient Spanish missions reminding all of its long and splendid history. It was marred, however, by the crowded, ramshackle homes of many poor Anglos, Mexicans, and Blacks. It was a city of warm romance and brutal battles.

San Antonio was a cosmopolitan blend of the easygoing affability of the Mexican, the industriousness of the German, garnished with a harsh layer of frontier Anglo violence. It was a town of small businessmen who provided medical, financial, and commercial services to most of southwest Texas and much of northern Mexico. A growing influence was the army's Fort Sam Houston and the growing numbers of air corps flying fields lacing the city.

During the daytime, in the warm, humid, sun-lit plazas people moved with deliberation, if not with languor. But when the sun dipped below the towers of San Fernando Cathedral, the pace quickened. Then the twang of country-western or the rhythms of the mambo rolled out from the myriad of illegal speakeasies where patrons lost their inhibitions and sometimes their lives after overly indulging in smuggled tequila, bootleg bourbon, or bathtub gin.

Excitement and danger came quickly to the young officer. One night while patrolling on the outskirts of San Antonio, a large hearse "going ninety miles an hour" sped by him. Johnny recounted, "I could see the coffin through the glass windows and it seemed they were in an awful hurry to get that man to a cemetery." Suspecting the coffin was filled with bathtub gin and rotgut whiskey, Johnny gunned his cycle and, after a wild chase, pulled up alongside the hearse driver, yelled, and motioned him to stop.

In response a gun was poked out of the window, and the man alongside the driver started shooting. Bullets whizzing about his head, Johnny braked, fell in behind the hearse, pulled his thumbbuster .45 from his holster, and promptly shot out both rear tires. The driver of the hearse fought the wheel of the wildly careening vehicle on the narrow road and finally succeeded in bringing it to a stop. Before he could wipe the sweat from his brow, he and his partner were looking down the barrel of Johnny's .45, and the young officer was not in a pleasant mood. Wisely they surrendered, and Johnny had made his first big arrest. The hearse, of course, was loaded with illegal booze.

At one time Johnny rode a relic of the 1930s, a motorcycle with a sidecar. His partner was Bill Hauck, who in later years would work many tough cases with him when he became chief constable of San Antonio's Precinct 1. In later years Hauck was elected sheriff of Bexar County.

In those days Johnny was a dapper-looking fellow, wearing starched khaki pants, white shirt, coat and tie, high-heeled cowboy boots, and a gray Stetson tilted rakishly over one eye. At six feet two inches, lean, with a clipped black mustache, he sent feminine hearts fluttering all over the courthouse.

The *San Antonio Evening News* gossip columnist once wrote, "Dapper Johnny Klevenhagen got the surprise of his life when a woman stopped him in the street and asked for his autograph. She said she thought he was John Boles, the movie actor. There is a resemblance too."

The footloose bachelor heartbreaker life, however, was about to end. In 1933, while the young lawman was taking a coffee break at the refreshment stand in the Bexar County Courthouse in San Antonio, he met up with the young lady with whom he would share his life.

As he sipped his black coffee, a pretty blonde girl named Viola Wolff, also taking a coffee break from her job as a telephone switchboard operator, approached the stand. A brief conversation soon turned into a romance, and on May 7, 1935, the two were married. If his personal life was flourishing, so was his reputation as a crack criminal investigator.

Klevenhagen's energy, savvy, and dedication to his work soon brought him to the attention of Will Wood, who, when he was elected constable of Precinct 1 in San Antonio in 1934, hired Johnny as deputy constable. It was in those early years that Johnny perfected his investigative techniques and not only made contacts among fellow police officers but also developed a rapport with those on the fringes of society: the hangers-on, the bar girls, petty crooks, and other sleazy characters that fluttered on the outskirts of criminal activity.

Johnny also acquired, among criminals, a reputation of a lawman who was very, very tough but who was also fair and would stand by his word. Unsavory though these people might be, throughout the years they were a vital source of information about criminal activity that enabled Johnny to break many difficult cases.

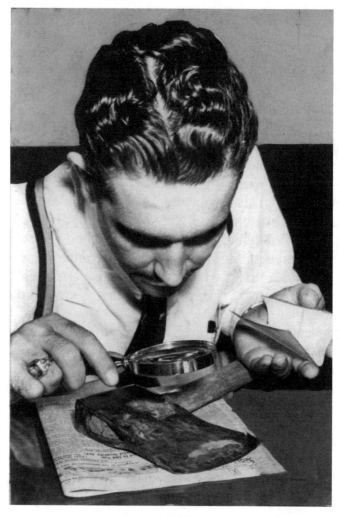

District Attorney Investigator Klevenhagen searches for a clue
while trying to solve a baffling San Antonio murder.

In 1936 Wood was elected sheriff of Bexar County and
brought Johnny with him as an investigator, and there was
plenty to investigate. The San Antonio economy was

wallowing in the depths of the country's worst depression, and criminal activity rose as the economy fell.

Police work, however, was not always bereft of humor. On a complaint from a puritanical church group, Johnny arrested a luscious twenty-eight-year-old blonde named Ruth Beaucaire for performing a "Parasol" dance at a Broadway Boulevard tavern. Testifying in her trial for indecent exposure, Johnny was asked by the prosecution to describe the dance.

"Well," he stammered, "Ruth wore a mask, a parasol, and a smile. Pretty soon she dropped the parasol. It's an art dance...I guess they call it."

When the laughter died, Ruth's fine was paid by the tavern owner, who gave his "Salome" a reassuring hug. The tavern owner's wife, however, was not amused. She sued her husband for divorce, charging he had had an affair with his "Salome." Johnny was soon after bigger game.

CHAPTER 2

The Red River Raider

At 9:30 on the sweltering morning of August 10, 1937, two well-dressed men stepped through the door of the cashier's office of the San Antonio Public Service Company bus garage in downtown San Antonio.

One of the men, chunky and florid-faced, carried a long cardboard box. The other, tall but slighter in build, blue-eyed and blond haired, was strikingly handsome. He was dressed in a white linen suit and wore a straw hat rakishly tilted over one eye. The two attracted little attention from the half dozen drivers and clerks lounging about the office, lazily chattering about baseball, cars, and women.

Suddenly the blond pulled a .45-caliber automatic pistol from his coat and in a loud, authoritative voice shouted, "This is a stickup. Stay quiet and you won't get hurt." At the same time the burly man opened the cardboard box revealing a twelve-gauge sawed-off shotgun and waved it at the group. The neighborly chattering quickly stopped, replaced by frightened stares as the men froze in place.

"Give me the money," the blond man said, pointing his pistol at the company's cashier. Frightened, the cashier pointed to a large chest filled with money bags containing more than $1,700 in nickels, dimes, quarters, and bus tokens, proceeds of the previous day's bus fares. The two men stuffed the coin bags in a larger bag and began backing out of the room. As they were leaving the blond said, "The money is insured isn't it." Then he laughed.

On their way out the burly man bumped into a bus driver coming off duty. "Hands up," he commanded. When the driver, H.H. Tessman, was too startled to move, the burly man struck him across the wrists with the shotgun barrel. Outside the building a black sedan with engine running awaited the two men, who slung the money sack into the back seat and jumped into the car while the driver gunned the engine and the vehicle sped down the street.

The cashier immediately telephoned the police, giving a partial description of the getaway car. At the same time the police dispatcher's office began receiving a blizzard of emergency calls. One reported an automobile accident with people injured only a few blocks from the holdup scene. The description of the car meshed with the cashier's description of the getaway car.

Simultaneously another call came in, and a man with a frantic voice almost incoherently described a holdup of the San Antonio Buick company at the other end of town. A third call described another downtown robbery. Within moments police cars were racing on fool's errands all over town. In the confusion the bandits made a clean getaway. Police Chief Owen W. Kilday later had to sheepishly admit to the press, "They duped us with phony calls." After the initial call, Klevenhagen and another deputy rushed to the bus garage. Talking to the cashier he got a complete description of the men and the last two numbers of the license of the getaway car.

Klevenhagen, over the years, had developed a mind like a computer memory bank. He had been in Houston several weeks back to pick up a prisoner, and while there he recalled a conversation with police officers about a blond bandit who had been driving them to a state of frenzy with a series of bold daylight robberies.

The Houston chief of detectives told him, "This guy has pulled a half dozen stickups and has gotten away with at least $50,000. We believe he killed a deputy sheriff in cold blood. He's also wanted for robbery in Galveston and Beaumont. He is a slippery son-of-a-bitch with an unfunny sense of humor. After every robbery he asks if the money is insured. Then he laughs." Before he returned to San Antonio, Klevenhagen had pocketed a mug shot of the man.

In a flash of insight, Klevenhagen asked the cashier, "Did the blond man say anything as he left with the money?" "Yes," the cashier answered, "He asked if the money was insured. Then he laughed." Klevenhagen let out a whoop, "I know who he is," he announced. To make sure, he drove to his office, retrieved the photo, and showed it to the men who had been in the bus barn office. All of the witnesses identified the man in the photo as the holdup man.

His name was Lawrence Rea. He was a thirty-one-year-old walking nightmare. He had been convicted of robbery with firearms in California and ensconced in San Quentin Prison for a number of years. Although he once attempted an unsuccessful jailbreak, for some strange reason known only to parole officers, he was let out on parole. Perhaps it was his mild-mannered, polite speech and good looks that convinced them he would become a good boy if released. It was a judgment that was to cost innocent lives.

In September 1935 Rea walked out of prison and immediately began a series of daring stickups. Like Pretty Boy Floyd and Baby Face Nelson, robbers and killers raised to the level of folk heroes, he had been raised wearing patched overalls in the dust ridden and poverty-stricken Oklahoma farmlands along the Red River.

When his identity became known, the press leaped on his story labeling Rea "The Ruthless Raider of the Red River." It was not only alliterative, it was true. Glorying in his reputation, he pulled a dozen robberies in California and left a trail of stickups and stolen cars from San Francisco to San Antonio. Although the FBI, Texas Rangers, and local police authorities in a dozen states were looking for him, he managed to elude them all. His taunt to his underworld cronies was, "They'll never take me alive."

It was of course one thing to identify Rae; it was another to catch him. Contrary to the Sherlock Holmes theory of detecting where minute clues lead you to the guilty, in the 1930s, when the forensic arts and fingerprinting were in their infancy, in practical police work it was developing contacts in the underworld that was most important in solving most cases.

For years Johnny had cultivated petty thieves, "happy girls," drug addicts, bartenders, cab drivers, tinhorn gamblers, and former bootleggers. Like all successful detectives he was a good actor and "con artist." He could play "good cop," dispensing understanding and sometimes even fixing minor charges.

He could also play a devastating "bad cop," and flashing his cold eyes on a culprit, tightening his jaw muscles, clenching his big fists, and spitting out threats, he could scare the hell out of even the most hardened criminal. After seven years as a police officer, Johnny could play underworld types like a symphony conductor. They would dance to the tune he played.

Aside from that, his lawman buddy Deputy Duke Carver said, "Klevenhagen was the handsome one.... Feminine hearts roll over and hum when he strolls by...and that is no handicap in the detective business." So suave, debonair Johnny Klevenhagen prowled the honky-tonk beer joints and dance halls of San Antonio's rough, tough west side. He didn't expect to find Rea, but as he tapped the informers or "stoolies" he had cultivated over the years, he did expect to find a lead.

He learned that Rea was a highly sexed self-styled Romeo who fancied that peculiar type of woman who found criminals fascinating. He flitted from one paramour to another like a crazed honeybee in a bed of roses. This was, Johnny thought, the chink in Rea's armor.

It was in the shank of the evening when Johnny strolled into a striptease joint called "La Vie Parisienne." There the nearly naked dancers gyrated under a bright spotlight to a hectic jazz beat, and the smoke hung so thick and the lights were so dim it was like feeling your way through a deep cave.

Through the gloom he spotted a heavily made up redhead, half bombed out of her mind on booze and drugs and babbling to a table full of sleazy women and cheap crooks. Her name was Patsy Burke, and she got her kicks by bedding down with thugs and stickup artists. She was loudly bragging about her "Larry," who she said was the most macho stud in town, "and he's poison when he's crossed." She boasted that after the bus garage robbery she had partied with him at the Gables Tourist Court.

As Klevenhagen sidled up behind her, she was mimicking Rae in a deep falsetto, "This is a stickup. Keep quiet and you won't get hurt. Anyway the money is covered by insurance." At that point Johnny rose from his chair behind her and said quietly, "Good evening, Patsy." He gave the rest of the party the patented Klevenhagen hard stare, and the others hurriedly left the table.

15

After Johnny discussed "accessory after the fact" and how many years in the "slammer" Patsy could receive, she gave up the name and address of one of Rea's accomplices, a man named Rudolph Smedley. At that Klevenhagen summoned backup and they rushed to the address, surprised Smedley, and took him to the county jail.

He was, in police jargon, a "good collar." He was wanted by Texas police for a series of robberies, and the FBI had a warrant out on him for possession of a sawed-off shotgun, a federal offense. The Bexar County Sheriff's Department charged him with robbery with firearms.

After intensive questioning and perhaps a promise of a reduced sentence, Smedley agreed to lead the lawmen to the elusive Rea. "He's got a new girlfriend in Austin," the former pal told them. The girl, a twenty-five-year-old "good looker" named Billie Morrison, was quickly located after a call to the Austin police. She lived in a small frame house on the outskirts of town.

Neighbors told police that Billie received a shadowy visitor on a number of nights. He came by auto, they said, driving to the back of her house with his headlights switched off. At this, the Austin police put Billie in custody and prepared a trap.

Since Rea bragged he would never be taken alive, the police expected a shootout. Armed with twelve-gauge shotguns loaded with double-ought buckshot and .45-caliber Thompson submachine guns, they surrounded the house and waited. Several officers took up positions inside the building. Their orders were simple, "Take no chances. If he goes for a gun, shoot to kill."

For two days and two nights they kept up the stakeout. Finally on the third night at four o'clock in the morning, the drowsy officers heard an auto approaching the house. As fingers tightened on weapons and officers sucked in their breaths, it pulled into the driveway. It came to a stop and a dim figure got out and walked to the back door of the house. "Billie, Billie," the figure whispered.

Travis County Sheriff Deputy Rip Collins, stationed inside, in his best falsetto whispered back, "Wait a minute." Rea paused a moment; another deputy threw a searchlight beam on him and yelled, "Hands up." But Rea ducked, pivoted, and ran toward the thick brush behind the house. Panting hard, a posse of lawmen crashed through the thickets after him, but they soon lost him in the murky light and heavy underbrush. Cursing, they realized he had escaped. Although at daylight and throughout the day they scoured the area, he was not to be found. "We should have gunned down the bastard," one officer murmured. Tragically they did not.

In Rae's abandoned automobile police found a rifle, pistol, and three sticks of dynamite. Also, empty moneybags from a San Antonio bank, change, and dozens of bus tokens were scattered on the floor of the car. While the police were calling in reinforcements and bloodhounds in an attempt to seal off the area, Rea raced through the rough country until he reached the small farming community of Govalle, a few miles southeast of Austin.

It was almost dawn on August 12 when Brad Payton, who owned a small farm, heard a prowler in his garage. Pulling on his overalls, he ran to the front door, which was being pounded by someone. Foolishly he opened the door.

Rea, wild-eyed and disheveled, stood in the doorway. He pointed a pistol at Payton's head and snarled, "Give me your car keys." Recklessly, Payton threw a punch at the bandit and Rea shot him through the heart. As he was bending over the dying farmer looking for keys, Payton's twenty-year-old son Norman, who leaped out of bed at the gunshot, stormed into the room. Seeing his bleeding father on the floor, he charged at Rea who then shot him in the groin.

Payton's wife was next. In a fury she threw herself on the intruder and grappled with him until he shot her in the stomach. Payton's other son, sixteen-year-old Leon, entered the room as his mother lay screaming on the floor. As Leon reached the man, he heard Norman gasping, "Give him the car keys." As Rea was prepared to gun down the last of the Paytons, Leon stopped, went to a bureau, and got the keys to the family automobile. Rea shoved his pistol into Leon's face and commanded, "Get in the car and drive."

Although half-hysterical with fear and grief, Leon started the car and drove down the country road for several miles. Suddenly Rea ordered him to stop. "I don't need you anymore, punk," he said, and he flung open the car door, kicked Leon out onto the road, and drove off. Leon stumbled several miles down the road until he came to the house of a nearby farmer, T.M. Markham, and screaming, beat on his door.

Sobbing hysterically, Leon blurted out the story of the attack. Markham grabbed the boy and led him to his automobile and sped to the Payton farmhouse where he found Brad dead and the other two bleeding badly. He telephoned the police immediately and within minutes mother and son were taken by ambulance to Brackenridge Hospital in Austin.

When Klevenhagen heard of Rea's murderous escape, he and Deputy Cyrus Heard loaded up a sheriff's automobile with twelve-gauge shotguns and a Thompson submachine gun and drove the eighty-five miles to Austin at eighty-five miles an hour. They also loaded a protesting and handcuffed Smedley into the back seat.

By the time they reached the Austin hospital, Norman had been stabilized and was able to talk. When

Klevenhagen showed him a picture of Rea, he groaned, "That's the man who killed my dad." There followed one of the greatest manhunts in Texas history with more than 200 peace officers including Texas Rangers, State Highway Patrolmen, sheriffs' deputies from two counties, and the city police of San Antonio, Austin, and Houston scouring underworld haunts in the search for Rea.

The San Antonio Public Service Board offered a $500 reward, and the state of Texas added another $500 for Rae's capture. In 1937 during the Depression years, $1,000 was a considerable amount of money.

During Klevenhagen's lengthy interrogation, Smedley gave up the address of a Houston hideout favored by Rea. Klevenhagen told Heard, "I believe he's holed up in Houston, we'll get him there. Let's go." The trio of two lawmen and one criminal piled in the car and burned up the highway. When they arrived at the Harris County sheriff's office, they received word that Payton's automobile had been found. The smashed-up vehicle was wrapped around a rail of a wooden plank bridge crossing a creek on the Weberville road fifteen miles southeast of Austin. Rea, traveling at high speed, apparently lost control when his tires hit the bridge's irregular planks and spun into the railing.

A small army of lawmen on horseback and on foot, leading bloodhounds, began combing the area. Unique for that time, a police airplane hedgehopped a few feet over the brush hoping for a sight of the fugitive. But Rea was still ahead of the game.

After searching the area proved futile, Klevenhagen told officers about Rea's possible hideout. It was reported to be an old farmhouse twenty miles northwest of Houston on a narrow dirt lane a few miles off the Hempstead road. Smedley told them the gang's signal was that if a truck was parked in the front yard it meant that Rea was in the house and that his auto was sheltered in a garage out back.

When Klevenhagen's posse arrived at the house, no truck was visible so the lawmen moved in quickly and netted two minor prizes. As they burst through the front door, they surprised an ex-convict associate of Rea's and a shapely young woman. In the house was an arsenal of sawed-off shotguns, rifles, automatic pistols, revolvers, and enough ammunition for a small battle.

They hauled the two off to jail then they staked out the house. This time they used enough men to make sure Rea would not again escape their trap. They waited hunkered down in the area for two days and nothing happened. Klevenhagen in disgust returned to Houston.

On a Sunday evening when Klevenhagen and the local lawmen were gloomily comparing notes and looking for new leads, another chapter of the operations of the now infamous "Red River Raider" came to light.

Three Houston businessmen, jabbering with excitement, barged into the office of the Houston chief of police with a frightening story. Fishing on the Colorado River, they decided to take a luncheon break, spread out a blanket, and laid out sandwiches, soft drinks, and other assorted snacks. They were sitting down to eat when a ragged stranger approached.

His face was scratched and his clothes were torn. Obviously he had been rushing through the tangled underbrush along the riverbank. He ran up to them, pointed a .45-caliber automatic pistol at the fishermen, and said, "You guys are driving me to Houston." Scooping up all the food, he forced the three men into the front seat while he got in the back with the sandwiches. "Drive," he ordered.

During the 150-mile trip little was spoken as Rea was too busy gobbling up a lunch for three. "He ate all our sandwiches," one of the fishermen complained, "and then he made us stop at a drive-in. He ordered a bunch of hamburgers and ate them as we drove."

Rea found an old pair of pants in the back seat and exchanged them for his brush-torn garment. He took a wide-brimmed sun hat from one of the men and a pair of dark sunglasses from another. On the outskirts of Houston he ordered the driver to stop, snarled, "Get the hell out of here," moved to the driver's seat, and sped off, leaving three very frightened Sunday fishermen standing by the side of the road.

After hiking to the nearest telephone, they called police and were picked up and taken to headquarters. Shown pictures of Rea, they identified him as the hungry stranger with the gun. When Johnny returned to headquarters to talk to the complaining men, he told them they were lucky that all they lost to a cold-blooded killer was an automobile and their lunch.

Within minutes after the fishermen had been taken home in police vehicles, an angry Houston cabdriver was brought in shouting that a man in a sun hat and dark sunglasses had shoved a gun in his face, took ten dollars from his wallet, and drove off in his cab. He too identified Rea from a photo as the man who had robbed him.

When one lead fails you try something else. From Smedley, Klevenhagen knew Rea was a sucker for betting on horses. He invariably lost most of his bets, which accounted for the frequency of his stickups. On this information police began to concentrate on known bookie joints. The following morning the stolen taxicab was located in the fashionable Westheimer section of the city. The officer who spotted the cab said the motor was still warm. This was the hottest lead yet.

Klevenhagen again questioned Smedley as to the location of bookie joints in the Westheimer district. But the felon had grown reluctant to talk. The repeated failures of San Antonio, Austin, and Houston police to arrest Rea had spooked him badly. He knew what the killer would do to someone who informed on him, and he shuddered at the thought.

After Klevenhagen pointed out that Smedley's best hope was Rea's arrest, he grudgingly gave him the name of a gambling hall in a private home in the Westheimer neighborhood.

Johnny rounded up an old girlfriend of the fugitive and had her telephone the gambling joint and ask for him. After a brief conversation the girlfriend, who was called "Frenchie," told the anxious officers, "He's there." Quickly a large, well-armed posse drove to the house and, guns drawn, crept up to the two-story residence.

By 11:45 that morning every door and window was covered by a submachine gun. This time there would be no escape. It was on this occasion that a lifelong friendship was formed between Houston Detective C.V. "Buster" Kern and Klevenhagen. In later years when Johnny was a captain in the Texas Rangers and Buster was sheriff of Harris County, the two would team up to wreak havoc on the Houston criminal world. But that was in the future.

That morning Buster had two tear gas grenades. He gave one to Johnny, and the two lawmen slipped up to the house. Kern threw the first grenade through the glass window, causing a drawn shade to roll up and revealing a startled Rea who quickly ducked out of sight. Johnny threw the second grenade and then the officers waited.

As clouds of tear gas roiled around inside the house, the cordon of police with fingers on their triggers waited for

Rea to come out shooting. Instead they heard a single shot and then silence.

After a few minutes went by, Kern produced two gas masks. He and Johnny donned them and with their automatics cocked they burst through the front door. Covering each other, they stalked through the cloud of tear gas until they had searched all of the ground floor. It was deserted.

They slowly edged up the stairs where there was less gas. If Rea was planning an ambush, it would be there. With hearts pounding and adrenaline flowing they reached the upstairs landing. They flung open a bedroom door expecting to receive a burst of gunfire. But there was only silence. Scattered on the floor were newspapers whose headlines blared of the massive police hunt. The smell of cordite mingled with the thinning gas fumes as they could see more clearly.

A pair of dark sunglasses and a wide brimmed sun hat hung on a chair. On a bed in the corner of the room lay a twelve-gauge shotgun. Nestled next to it was the body of Lawrence Rea. He had held the gun to his chest, squeezed the trigger, and died instantly from the blast that tore through his heart.

Under his pillow was a cocked .45 automatic. In his pockets were two dollars in nickels and dimes. There were a dozen bus tokens spilled on the floor. After robberies that hauled in an estimated $100,000, he died broke. Only the bookies had gotten rich. In a vain effort to elude recognition, he had dyed his eyebrows and hair black.

Police later caught a twenty-year-old punk who drove the San Antonio getaway car. He and Smedley both received long prison sentences. They never found out who made the phony police calls.

As they were standing over the body of the very dead "Red River Raider," Kern said, "I thought he would put up a fight." With a sigh of relief Johnny said, "So did I."

CHAPTER 3

The Bridegroom Bank Bandit

On March 2, 1938, in a brief ceremony in Laredo, Texas, Harry Northcutt was married to a pretty young student at nearby Kingsville College, whose name will not be revealed.

The groom at six feet, one hundred eighty pounds, with wavy blond hair and a twinkle in his sky blue eyes was the stuff of a young girl's dream. He was, he said, from a prosperous family prominent in the oil and gas business. And although she had known him for only a short time, he was a man whose charm, exquisite good manners, and seemingly good humor more than matched his Hollywood good looks, and she was deeply in love with him.

After a brief three-day honeymoon, Harry left his bride at the home of some relatives in Runge, Texas, saying he had business to conduct for his father in north Texas. He kissed his bride good-bye, waved farewell, said he would be back soon, and drove away.

There were, however, a few facts unknown to the young lady. The real name of her twenty-five-year-old Adonis was Selvie Winfield Wells, and he had a long history as an

outlaw. He first was sent to jail as a teenager for commit-
ting a robbery, and after being granted a parole he moved
to Camden, Arkansas, where he kidnapped and robbed a
prominent physician, leaving him stranded in the woods
after he took the doctor's wallet and automobile.

He was soon caught and in November 1933 was sentenced to fifteen years in the Arkansas state prison. Four
years later on January 14, 1938, he managed to escape and
make his way to Texas.

The business trip that interrupted his honeymoon
included a plan to rob a bank in the small but prosperous
little central Texas town of Luling. Luling in the 1870s had
been a cattle center, and when the railroad came through it
prospered. Then in 1922 after wildcatters made a big oil
strike nearby, it became a boomtown. For a while it was
known as "the toughest town in Texas," but more than a
decade later it had settled down into a drowsy small town
routine.

Wells had planned on that routine, for shortly after
noon on March 5, when he knew most of the employees of
the Citizens State Bank were out to lunch and few if any
customers would be doing business, he sauntered into the
bank. He approached the two lady tellers and in a soft,
quiet voice told them, "I'm robbing your bank, please don't
give me any trouble." They didn't and Wells moved behind
the counter and began stuffing bills and coins from the cash
drawers into a paper sack. One of the tellers later told
police she saw the butt of a pistol sticking out of his shirt.

After he cleaned out all the cash drawers, he told the
tellers to open the bank vault, but they claimed they didn't
have the combination and that he would have to wait for a
bank officer to come back from lunch. Wells smiled,
shrugged his shoulders, and prepared to wait. When a

customer entered the bank, however, he suddenly left, walked to his parked automobile, and drove off.

As he drove away both tellers ran into the street yelling, "He robbed the bank. He robbed the bank." An alert bystander scribbled down the license number of the fleeing automobile and notified police. The tellers described the bandit as wearing hand-tooled cowboy boots, a big wide-brimmed Stetson, khaki shirt, and blue trousers. Around his neck he was wearing a kerchief with a horseshoe design.

Importantly, one of the tellers noticed that on his left wrist he had a tattoo of a red eagle holding a green snake in its mouth. To the Luling police this was the best clue yet. Although most lawbreakers apparently don't realize it, police love tattoos. Probably that's one reason why tattoo artists ensconced in state prisons are allowed, if not encouraged, to practice their art. For many convicts out of boredom, a desire to appear tough, or to make some sort of statement ranging from "Love," "Mom," "Death before dishonor" or whatever stray thoughts wander through their flummoxed minds, decorate their arms, wrists, and hands with tattoos. As a result many police departments keep a record of tattoos filed alongside photographs and fingerprints.

While the tellers seemed a little charmed by the very polite bandit, the bank officers wailed that he got away with more than $3,000, not a bad haul for Depression-wracked Texas. A few days later police found the getaway car, which had been stolen the day before the robbery, abandoned, and burned on the shoulder of a lonely county road. The sole clue they had was the tattoo.

Luling police soon notified nearby sheriffs' offices and state police of Wells' description. When the information reached Klevenhagen, he reached back into his mental file cabinet of criminals and then started calling on his many "contacts," that being a euphemism for sweating stool pigeons. Finally, an old ex-convict recalled a fellow convict named Wells, a native of Caldwell, Texas, who had a red eagle tattoo.

Klevenhagen phoned in the tip to Luling police; however, a red herring had sent them off on another tangent. Then a student from Texas A&M University at Bryan, Texas, was hitchhiking home near Austin when he was picked up by a young fellow driving a blue Chrysler. The blond-haired, blue-eyed, personable young driver told the Aggie his name was Harry Northcutt, the son of a local oilman.

The car radio was tuned to some cowboy music, according to the Aggie, when a news flash came on describing the Luling bank robber. While the physical description fit Northcutt, he thought little of it, but when it was mentioned the bank robber wore a kerchief with horseshoe decorations on it and he noticed that Northcutt was wearing a similar kerchief, he became both suspicious and somewhat scared. The Aggie told the driver he lived in Luling and needed to take another road to get home. Wells/Northcutt obligingly let him off, waving a cheery good-bye. When the Aggie got to Luling, he immediately went to police headquarters and told of his suspicions.

Meanwhile, Luling police had tracked down the bride of Northcutt living in Karnes City, Texas, but soon determined she was a naive, trusting young lady who was soon to suffer a broken heart when she learned the truth about her husband. And they believed her when she said she didn't remember where he was staying during his business trip.

The Aggie hitchhiker cleverly had written down the license number of the blue Chrysler, and a statewide alert was put out on the automobile. Johnny Klevenhagen, meanwhile, learned from an informer that Wells often used the pseudonym of Northcutt, thus clearing up the confusion. Now, they knew exactly who they were looking for.

On Saturday, March 12, local lawmen spotted Wells' automobile leaving a Beeville restaurant. Bee County Chief Deputy Sheriff R.J. Bell and Beeville Chief of Police Patrick Martin attempted to curb Wells' car, but the bandit spotted them and gunned the Chrysler, driving northeast on State Highway 12, now U.S. Highway 59. Giving chase, the two were unable to pass the speeding Chrysler. As Martin drove, Bell got on the radio to try to set up roadblocks on all roads leading north or east.

Deputy Bell, leaning out of the window, opened fire at the speeding car finally blowing out a rear tire. Wells, hitting speeds over ninety miles per hour, desperately fought the wheel as the auto careened to the right, nearly going into a ditch. But he still had enough control to swerve back to the left and regain the highway, finally jamming on the brakes and coming to a tire burning, screeching stop.

As Martin pulled up beside the Chrysler, Bell leaped from the car and yelled, "Hands up." Wells replied by opening fire with his pistol, shooting the thirty-seven-year-old deputy in the left hand, left leg, and thigh. Before Bell lapsed into shock he got off one shot, hitting the bandit in the left foot. Wells, however, turned to Martin and shot the sixty-year-old police chief, who was still behind the wheel of his car. His bullet struck the lawman in the chest but luckily was deflected by a bone and spun into his left shoulder, missing his heart.

Then Wells limped to the lawman's automobile, jerked the bleeding, semiconscious Martin from behind the wheel and threw him into the street. He took the officers' pistols and a shotgun, got into their auto, and drove off. Fortunately, within a few minutes a passing motorist saw the two officers lying in the roadway, stopped, hauled them into his car, and rushed them to the Beeville hospital. On the wounded officers' directions, he alerted police that Wells was still driving north on Highway 59.

As Wells was speeding along the south Texas coastal bend, lawmen from all over central and southeast Texas were setting up roadblocks on every highway and country road heading north. Wells, driving 100 miles an hour in the stolen patrol car, covered 115 miles to Wharton, Texas, before he ran into a massive roadblock manned by sheriff's deputies, local police, and state highway patrolmen.

Spotting the police cars parked across the highway, Wells careened off the road onto the shoulder, his right wheels momentarily sinking into the dirt, then spinning out and driving the car back onto the highway, skirting the roadblock as police desperately opened fire on the speeding auto. There followed a forty-mile chase with lawmen firing more than fifty rounds, riddling the stolen patrol car but missing Wells and failing to slow him down.

The bandit raced through the small towns of Wharton, Hungerford, Kendleton, and Beasley, miraculously avoiding killing other motorists and terrified pedestrians. When a Wharton deputy pulled his car up close, Wells twisted around and fired a shot that struck the shoulder of the police officer, causing him to break off the chase.

Two miles west of Rosenberg, before the highway turns into a Houston freeway, frantic police had constructed a massive roadblock that covered the road from shoulder to shoulder. There would be no hotshot dodging around this time.

Heavy traffic in the area caused a backup of hundreds of confused motorists, honking and cursing as they were stopped by police and required to sit in their overheating cars as the officers grimly waited for Wells to arrive. When Wells approached the block he could see there would be no end run this time. But charging ahead, he aimed at the right side of the road, and as police leaped to the side, fearing he was going to try and smash through, Wells slammed on the brakes, stopping just before he was about to hit the line of blocking autos.

Flinging open his car door, with a shotgun in one hand and a pistol in the other, Wells blasted away with both guns. Dodging a hail of police bullets, he leaped over the hood of a police car and ran past the roadblock, turning and firing as he ran.

Stopped in the left-hand traffic lane fifty yards from the roadblock, motorist Frank Albright wondered why traffic was jammed up. There must be a bad wreck up ahead he was thinking when suddenly there was the screaming of brakes applied at high speed followed by a burst of gunfire with rifles, shotguns, and heavy caliber pistols blasting away in what seemed like a small battle.

Then he saw a man running toward him along the shoulder. He saw him stop, turn, and fire two shots at pursuing men in uniform. Within a few seconds the man was panting by the side of his automobile. He jammed his pistol in his belt and, pointing his shotgun at Albright's head, yelled, "Get the hell out of the car."

As the motorist momentarily froze, Wells jerked open the car door, dragged him from behind the wheel, and flung him out onto the road. Jumping behind the wheel, Wells spun the auto around, pushed the gas pedal to the floor, and roared off toward Houston.

Before the police could start their cars and pursue, Wells managed to lose them in the heavy Houston traffic. He had fought three gun battles in over 150 miles of raging pursuit, wounded three police officers, and was still free and running wild.

Two days later on March 14, police officers found Albright's automobile in a pasture outside of Houston. While most of the intensive manhunt for Wells centered in the south Texas area, Johnny Klevenhagen learned something different. Remembering that Wells had escaped from an Arkansas prison, he started hunting 200 miles further north. Making inquiries among the many ex-convicts he had befriended or at least played square with, he finally contacted an underworld character who told him Wells often used a small farmhouse three miles north of the small northeastern town of Gladewater, Texas, not too far from the Arkansas border. It was also close to Shreveport, Louisiana, and its sister town of Bossier City where in its honky-tonks, unlike dry north Texas, there was free flowing booze, gambling, and young ladies of ambivalent virtue.

Johnny put out further feelers into the Bossier City underworld and found out that Wells had lost hundreds of dollars there on booze, broads, slot machines, and horses. He then alerted the Gladewater police as well as other law enforcement agencies, and soon a massive posse of FBI agents, sheriffs' deputies from five Texas counties, local city police officers, and Texas Rangers began to converge at Gladewater.

At one o'clock in the morning of March 16, a long line of police cars carrying dozens of armed-to-the-teeth law officers snaked along a narrow road north of Gladewater. They halted a mile from a small wooden farmhouse and then on foot proceeded silently in single file toward the house.

Klevenhagen said a full moon lit up the eerie fields and bathed them in such a soft glow that they did not need flashlights to creep up on the house. They could see an automobile parked in the rear of the wooden cabin; Wells was at home. Quietly they surrounded the dwelling, took cover, then cocked the Thompson submachine guns, heavy caliber rifles, and shotguns and waited. This time there would be no escape for Harry Wells.

Perhaps because he had given the authorities the tip that led them there, Johnny pretty much led the posse. He took a tear gas grenade from the trunk compartment of his auto, nodded to the partly concealed officers, and bending over in a crouch he jogged twenty-five yards across a field and came up to a bedroom window.

Crouching under the window, his harsh yell broke the silence as he shouted, "Wells, come out with your hands up." When there was no reply, again he yelled, "Wells, come out with your hands up." Again no reply. Johnny raised up, pulled the pin on the tear gas grenade, and with a mighty heave, threw it at the windowpane.

The sound of the breaking glass gave way to fearful curses as Wells coughed and snorted and the billowing gas spread throughout the house. The gas burned his eyes and half-blinded him. Again Johnny shouted, "Wells, come out with your hands up."

The bandit made a half-strangled reply, "Are you going to shoot?" he cried. Johnny hollered, "Not if your hands are grabbing air." At that, coughing and with great tears streaming down his cheeks, Harry Wells flung open the door of the house and came out with his empty hands grabbing air. Inside the house the police found a pistol, rifle, and shotgun and a few hundred rounds of ammunition. Wells was promptly cuffed and driven to the Gladewater jail where more than a dozen police agencies argued about who should try him first.

Of the $3,000 he took from the Luling bank, only $1,000 was recovered; the rest Wells said was lost gambling and whoring in Louisiana. He did, however, buy a new ten-gallon cowboy hat, a bright silk shirt, and new pair of cowboy boots since his earlier pair was ruined when the Beeville policeman's bullet hit him in the left foot.

Wells talked freely to police and a bevy of newspaper reporters who interviewed him in his cell. He jokingly told police officers, "I had been drinking before I pulled that bank job in Luling. That only goes to show you, never drink on the job."

He admitted his biggest mistake was shooting the two Beeville police officers. "That really put the heat on me," he grinned. Wells was lucky that all three police officers he wounded recovered because if one had died, he probably would have kept a date with the Texas prison system's electric chair.

His major regret was, "I wish I wasn't the kind of guy I am. I married a swell girl, and I'm sorry I was not the kind of man she thought I was. She was studying to be a teacher and didn't know I was an ex-con. She thought I was pretty keen. She knew I drank and gambled but that was all. I guess she thinks different now. I heard she is going to leave school because of all of this, and that is what makes me sorry and sad. I figured on moving us out of Texas and settling down for a new start in life after I picked up a few nickels, but...," he shrugged.

Wells was later sued by the National Surety Corporation for the amount of the unrecovered bank loot. It was a lawsuit that brought a grin to Johnny Klevenhagen, who remarked, "A Texas district court judge sentenced Wells to ninety-nine years for the robbery of a filling station shortly before he pulled the Luling bank robbery; then he was convicted of the bank robbery in a federal district court and the judge sentenced him to spend ninety-nine years in Alcatraz. I expect it will be some little time before they are able to collect."

CHAPTER 4

Alligator Joe

It began in the summer of 1938 when an old Mexican field hand named Manuel sidled up to Bexar County Deputy Sheriff John Gray who, on his day off, was hunting doves near Elmendorf, Texas, a small farming town some seventeen miles southwest of San Antonio.

It had been a hardworking community of 300 mostly peopled by descendants of German immigrants. During the years of Prohibition, however, it had gotten a bad reputation as a hangout for bootleggers and assorted thugs. Since then the Bexar County Sheriff's Department had kept a jaundiced eye on some of its more unsavory characters.

Manuel, Gray knew, was no fool and had something on his mind, so he listened as the old man whispered, "Follow me," and led the deputy to a small, isolated clearing near the San Antonio River. There, Manuel told him that Hazel Brown, a waitress who had befriended him and given him a meal when he was broke and a cool drink of water on a hot day, had been missing for more than a week.

Hazel, a pretty, young twenty-three-year-old woman worked at Joe Ball's Tavern. Joe was a man with a shady reputation who was under suspicion by police as a bootlegger and as a fence for stolen automobile parts.

"No one will tell me what happened to my friend Hazel," Manuel recounted. "And funny," he said, "Joe Ball's wife has also vanished. He is a bad man, maybe he fed those women to his alligators."

The deputy pointed out that waitresses often get fed up and quit, particularly after working in a dump like the tavern and for a surly bastard like Joe. Besides, he said, his wife is probably off visiting relatives.

"There is more," Manuel said nervously. "Last night I am drinking with my cousin, Juan, down by the river. About midnight I was going home and passed by the house of Joe Ball's sister, Mrs. Loap, and I saw a man moving a great big barrel. This barrel has one terrible stink. It smells like something dead is inside; maybe Hazel and Mrs. Ball. Please tell no one what I have told you."

Gray humored the man, saying he would keep silent but would investigate the mysterious barrel. Maybe, he thought, Manuel was drinking too much tequila and his imagination had gone loco. But in the case of Joe Ball anything was possible, although nothing had ever been proven. The tavern was a wooden shack where Joe sold beer and where the surrounding riffraff gathered to get sloppy drunk on Friday and Saturday nights. Also, there were the alligators. In a large fenced pit behind his shabby bar there were half a dozen of the large, ill-tempered reptiles. Joe called them his pets. He fed them dead cats and dogs according to some neighbors. Others said it was live cats and dogs. The area did stink badly, although that didn't seem to bother the tavern's clientele.

In fact, it was known locally that every Saturday night when his customers were more than half drunk, they would all sally out by the alligator pit and toss in any wild animal, possum, squirrel, chicken, or household pet. Hooting and hollering, they watched the 'gators gobble them up. When that fun was over they went back to the bar where often Ball held cockfights.

When Gray returned to San Antonio he mentioned his conversation with Manuel to Sheriff Will Wood. He responded, "It's quiet for a change. Get Klevenhagen and go back and check it out. You never know."

The following day Klevenhagen and Gray met with Elton Cude, also a deputy. Cude said he had been investigating an auto theft in Elmendorf. Naturally, while he was there he gave Joe's beer joint a close look. "I saw the barrel. It was a fifty-five-gallon gasoline drum. It stunk like hell."

On the following Saturday Klevenhagen and Gray drove to Elmendorf and pulled up alongside the tavern. Entering the dim building they were tempted to hold their breath. The floors were dirty and the place reeked of the smell of stale beer. Corrugated iron shutters sealed out sunlight, making it difficult to see through the cigarette smoke that hung like a pall in the barroom. The walls were covered with pasted-up pictures of naked women cut out of magazines.

Although it was not quite noon, Joe's customers—Anglos, Blacks, and Hispanics—were busily getting drunk. They were a scurvy-looking lot, and they avoided eye contact as the two lawmen entered the barroom.

Klevenhagen asked the bartender if Joe Ball was around. He got a sullen "No." Is Hazel Brown here? he was asked. Again a curt "No." Klevenhagen asked two waitresses the same questions. He got furtive glances from Johnie Lowe and Margie Casbeer. "Don't let Joe know we were talking to you. He might get mad and fire us," Johnie said. They both denied knowing the whereabouts of the missing women. "They just aren't around anymore," Margie said.

A neighbor, Elton Fullerton, was more friendly. He said one day both women were just "gone." He added there was another waitress who had suddenly vanished. Her name, he said, was Big Minnie. He didn't know her last name. He said, "Back in June 1937 she had been working at the tavern and then she disappeared."

The two detectives left, and after looking around the area they returned to the tavern. "Ball in yet?" Johnny asked. The bartender nodded, "In back." Striding to a storeroom in back of the place, the two lawmen found Ball stacking beer cases.

He looked like someone the MGM casting office would cast as an evil villain. Stocky, muscular, with bulging biceps, sweat pouring down a dirty shirt, he had a broad chest and close cropped hair topping a square face. Ball had small, squinty pig-like eyes and yellow snaggled teeth. When he attempted a rare smile it resembled a picture of a hungry shark.

As Johnny began to identify himself, Ball snapped, "I know who you are. What do you want?"

"We heard your wife is missing. Maybe you can tell us where she is?"

"I don't know. She left three or four months ago. I think she went to visit relatives."

"You don't know where."

Ball shrugged.

It was a rather casual answer for a missing wife. Johnny asked, "What happened to Hazel Brown?"

"She quit. I don't know where she went."

"Mind if we look around?" Johnny asked. Ball's reply was an affirmative grunt.

As they stepped out the back door, the two detectives were attacked by a swarm of black flies gathered around a pile of rotting garbage. Ball following them out, walked to the concrete alligator pit, drew some putrid meat from a bag, and tossed it into the foul greenish-black water. Suddenly a half dozen large alligators thrashed and churned in an acrobatic frenzy as they fought over the chunks of meat.

As Klevenhagen and the other deputy watched in disgust, Ball smirked, "Nice fellows aren't they?" Both detectives got the distinct feeling Ball would prefer to be feeding them to his pets.

Johnny asked Ball, "Where is that big steel barrel you had back here?" With considerable irritation Ball replied, "I don't have any steel barrel. What's this all about?"

"We're looking for Hazel Brown," Johnny replied, "and we intend to find out what happened to her."

"I told you I don't know. She just quit."

By now Johnny's intuition was setting off alarm bells. He believed there was something terribly wrong about Ball and his entire setup. As Ball returned to the tavern, Johnny suggested that the two lawmen visit Ball's sister. They walked across the road to Mrs. Loap's frame house. When she answered the door, Johnny introduced himself and his deputy and then asked, "Where is that steel barrel that Joe had over here a few days ago?"

The woman replied, "I don't know where it is. Joe had it over here and it stunk so bad I made him move it."

That did it. The man was lying. For what reason? Johnny believed he had probable cause to take Joe into custody for a siege of intensive questioning. The two lawmen returned to the tavern, and as Ball watched sullenly, they searched the place from one end to another. But they found nothing.

Klevenhagen confronted Ball, "You are under arrest."

"For what reason?"

"Suspicion."

"Suspicion of what?"

"Suspicion is enough for now."

For a moment Ball's facial muscles twitched and he seemed poised to attack. Then he gave his twisted smile and said, "Okay, but let me count the money in the cash register first."

When Klevenhagen nodded he went behind the bar, opened the register, withdrew the money, and pocketed a miscellany of bills and change. Then he went to an ice chest, pulled out a bottle of beer, uncapped it, and poured it into a dirty glass. "One for the road," he grimaced. He had gulped half the glass when it happened.

From behind the counter he pulled out a .45-caliber automatic pistol. There are two versions of what happened next. One version says he pointed the gun at his own body and pulled the trigger.

Deputy Gray, however, said Ball raised the pistol to kill Klevenhagen, but "Johnny drew and shot so fast that I could hardly see him move. It was just a blur."

Johnny fired his .45 a millisecond before Ball's pistol went off. The bullet from Johnny's gun struck Ball in the neck and ripped out his throat. Ball was apparently thrown back by the impact. As his arm was jerked up, his gun went off, and his own bullet went in under his chin and blew out his brains.

A coroner later reported a verdict of suicide. "If Ball shot himself it was suicide. If Ball pulled a gun on Johnny Klevenhagen, that also is suicide." It was the beginning of the Johnny Klevenhagen legend.

There remained, however, the mystery of what had happened to Mrs. Ball, Hazel Brown, and some poor woman named Big Minnie. Other neighbors and some of the bar patrons told Johnny that over the years several other young waitresses who worked at the tavern had suddenly vanished. Johnny thought of the alligators and shuddered.

Klevenhagen soon located Ball's brother, who said Joe told him that his wife, Dolores, had gone to San Diego, California. A missing persons report was sent to the San Diego police. Dolores would not be hard to locate; she had only one arm. "The alligators?" Johnny wondered.

The riffraff at the bar were all questioned to no avail. When Johnny started questioning a tall, massively built African American named Clifton Wheeler, the man suddenly volunteered, "I'm sure glad that man's dead." When Wheeler, who had been a handyman around the tavern for many years, was asked about his elation, the thirty-two-year-old man replied, "I was afraid of him. I was afraid he would kill me. I knew too much. I could talk and send him to jail. I thought he was going to shoot me. He was a real devil."

Johnny had a hunch there was more to it than just a knowledge of petty crimes. After intense questioning, Johnny leaned over the man and barked, "What happened to Hazel Brown?"

With a heavy sigh, Wheeler bowed his head and blurted out, "Ball clubbed her to death. He also shot her in the head. He stuffed her in a big gasoline barrel. Then he made me load it in his truck. We took it to the river and dumped it in. He made me do it. He would have killed me if I didn't help."

By this time the coroner, several other deputies armed with shovels, and a number of newspapermen arrived on the scene. Although it was getting dark, Johnny told Wheeler, "Take us to that spot on the river." The big man agreed and the group of men wended their way along the San Antonio Riverbank. They had hiked and stumbled about three miles along the brush-filled bank when Wheeler held up his hand and said, "This here's the place."

They were standing on a bluff about one hundred yards from the river. "Are you sure this is the spot?" Johnny asked. The big man nodded. "Nonsense," Johnny exploded with exasperation, "Even you can't toss a barrel with a body in it a hundred yards." Wheeler heaved another sigh, rolled his eyes, and said, "I ain't been telling the truth."

Klevenhagen realized the man was not only scared but that he was also partly demented. In simple terms he told Wheeler he was now in big trouble and could go to jail for years after admitting he was an accessory to a cold-blooded murder. Finally he asked, "Why the hell did you lie to us?"

By now the confused band of body hunters was beginning to stumble around on the rather creepy riverbank as a full moon began to peek out of the clouds. It seemed like a scene from a grade B vampire movie.

"Boss," the big man shuddered, "It's too dark here. Let's do this in the morning."

"We'll do it now and I want the truth now," Johnny commanded. He sent several deputies back to the automobiles to bring up flashlights. Wheeler finally fessed up. "The lady wasn't in the barrel when I threw it in the river. We buried her right here."

When the deputies returned, Wheeler said he had dug a hole about seven feet deep and three feet wide. With all the flashlights turned on, two deputies started to dig. Johnny grabbed the third shovel and shoved it into Wheeler's hands, "Dig," he commanded.

The men dug for several hours until the flashlight batteries burned out. Klevenhagen built a fire out of brush, and the flames leaped into the air casting grotesque shadows in the flickering light. Then a shovel full of dirt tossed out of the hole gave out a stomach-turning stink. They knew then that Wheeler had not lied. They next hit a layer of bricks. The deputies climbed out of the hole and Wheeler removed the bricks one by one, exposing the body.

Fighting against retching from the horrible smell, Johnny tossed a rope to Wheeler who wrapped it around the body, and the lawmen pulled it to the surface. It was a woman's torso, but the arms, legs, and the head were missing. "My God," someone muttered.

Wheeler rummaged around the hole and handed up a leg, another leg, then an arm, then another arm. "We've found Hazel Brown," Johnny said. "Dolores Ball has only one arm, and Minnie's been gone for over a year." The putrid, gelatinous mess of guts and blood had to be a recent killing. It had to be Hazel.

Johnny went over to a filthy, smelly, shaken Wheeler, "Where's her head?" he demanded. The big man said they had cooked the head and clothes over a fire. He pointed to a smelly nearby pile of ashes. It was almost all that was left of Hazel Brown. Combing the fire site, Johnny found a few teeth, some small cranial bones, and a silver shoe buckle.

"What did he cut her up with?" Johnny asked.

"An axe, then a meat saw."

"Why did he kill her?"

"He said she knew too much."

"About what?"

"Don't know, Boss."

Klevenhagen was still concerned about the fate of Dolores Ball and the girl named Big Minnie. He noticed that Wheeler seemed more agitated than ever. After they arrived back at the city and Wheeler was escorted to a county cell, Johnny asked, as the door slammed shut, "What else do you have to tell me?"

Wheeler pursed his lips, "Well, Boss, there was the boy and the other lady. She was named Big Minnie and was one of the barmaids."

My God, Johnny thought, how many more corpses are going to turn up? "What about Dolores Ball?"

Wheeler denied any knowledge of what happened to Dolores or to a sixteen-year-old boy. The boy, he said, was a constant companion to Ball. Then, according to Wheeler, he just disappeared.

"I know about Minnie, though," he said, "her full name was Minnie Gotthardt. She was a waitress at the tavern."

Then it came spilling out like water from a faucet. "She's buried near Corpus Christi Bay near Ingleside. I was with Ball when he killed her. It was on the beach. We all went swimming then Ball sent me after whiskey. I brought it back and we drank it raw.

"Ball pointed to some sea gulls and said 'Look there, Minnie.' When she turned he shot her through the head. Then he hit her with a club to make sure she was dead. Then we buried her in the sand. I know how to find her, Boss."

Since it had already been a twenty-hour day, Johnny told the others to go home and get some sleep. Leaving Wheeler in his cell, the weary lawmen returned to their homes and in an uneasy sleep may have dreamed of alligators munching on Dolores Ball and an unknown sixteen-year-old boy. The next morning they again would go grave digging.

Although the next morning was Sunday, Johnny with an entourage of deputies, newspaper reporters, photographers, and Wheeler in tow, revisited the tavern at Elmendorf. Some of the party shuddered as they viewed the alligators, who were agitated because they hadn't been fed.

Klevenhagen found the axe in the rear of the tavern matted with blood and human hair. The alligators were taken out of the pit by reptile handlers from the San Antonio Zoo where they found a permanent if less exciting home. The pit was drained as part of an intensive search for other murder victims, but no other bodies were found. The barrel and the meat saw were fished out of the river by firemen. A coroner's report stated that Hazel had been beaten and then shot through the heart, hopefully before she was dismembered.

The following Monday, Dolores Ball was located in San Diego by the local police. She said she fled Elmendorf because of her fear her husband would kill her. No one doubted her story.

On Tuesday morning the usual entourage drove two hundred miles to Ingleside on the Gulf of Mexico where they were greeted by San Patricio County sheriff's deputies and another bevy of reporters and photographers. As Wheeler led them through the shifting white sands on the beach, the hot, humid weather soon had them sweat-soaked and sun blistered.

Finally Wheeler pointed to a large dune near a tree with a broken branch. "We buried her here," he said. Shovels were passed out and Wheeler and several deputies began to dig. They dug all afternoon with pick and shovels but made little progress as the sliding sands filled in the hole as fast as they dug it out.

Toward twilight Johnny called a halt. He agreed they were wasting their time, and he said he would arrange to get a large power shovel and they would try again. Klevenhagen returned to San Antonio to meet with Dolores Ball. She, however, could shed no light on the disappearance of Minnie, the teen-aged boy, or other female waitresses who were rumored to have also disappeared.

Johnny and a colleague attempt to locate the body of "Big Minnie" who was buried in the sand on a beach near Ingleside.

It wasn't until the morning of October 13 that the Texas State Highway Department arrived at the beach site with a huge gasoline-driven shovel. The big shovel, the lawmen, and the swarms of press attracted a large crowd of gawkers who were both thrilled and frightened at the thought of seeing a woman's murdered body torn out of the sand.

The sightseers had to be ordered back several times as they crowded near the hole, causing sand to slide back in and slow the digging process. It became a carnival atmosphere as some of the spectators brought beach umbrellas, picnic lunches, and an untold number of box cameras. Swarms of children ran and screamed, playing cops and robbers around the dunes.

Klevenhagen, left, supervises the dig which finally located the body of "Big Minnie," a victim of "Alligator Joe."

It was almost four o'clock in the afternoon and the big shovel had dug a hole more than twenty feet deep and ten feet wide, when a load of sand was scooped up and a human head became visible.

Klevenhagen jumped into the hole and began clearing away sand when the sides caved in and buried him up to his armpits with Minnie's remains. After much straining and cursing he was pulled up out of the sandy grave. Scrambling back into the hole with shovels, the deputies dug out the decomposing body of Minnie Gotthardt. There was a bullet hole on the left side of her head.

An ambulance soon arrived and the driver brought out some canvas bags. Klevenhagen, with Minnie's head on his shovel, filled the first bag, and the other deputies shoveled out other parts until the whole body was removed.

Detectives were still puzzled over the motive for the slaying. Klevenhagen, however, gave the tavern a thorough search and found a letter written by Minnie to Ball. In it she threatened revenge on Ball, who she said dumped her for another woman. An autopsy later revealed she was seven months pregnant when she was killed. She said she would

Searching for the body of a murder victim,
Johnny is helped up from a collapsed trench on the Gulf beach.

give information to the police that would send her betrayer to jail.

Minnie's body was not claimed, and she was buried in a paupers field at Aransas Pass, a small fishing village on the Gulf Coast.

Klevenhagen believed Minnie knew about Ball's operations as a fence for stolen automobiles and the tavern owner killed her to shut her up. Why Ball killed Hazel Brown was never determined, nor was the possible fate of the missing teenage boy or the other rumored missing women. Neighbors believed Ball fed them to his alligators, but nothing was ever proved.

Wheeler, who was sentenced to two years in the state penitentiary, probably told all he knew. As to the fate of the others, the alligators knew, but they weren't talking.

CHAPTER 5

With the Rangers

In 1940 Will Wood ran for re-election as sheriff of Bexar County, and Johnny campaigned hard for his boss. Wood unfortunately had a temper problem, particularly when encountering nosy newspaper reporters. Once during the campaign when a reporter continued to press him about producing some records, the sheriff yelled, "I am now going to kick the shit out of you," and lunged at the man. Fortunately Johnny got between him and his quarry, and a First Amendment case was avoided.

But perhaps Wood's temper was contagious. A short time later, while Johnny was politicking for his boss in the courthouse corridor, a "ward heeler" working for the opposition candidate made several loud remarks about the supposed canine antecedents of Wood and Klevenhagen. In reprisal, Johnny slapped the man in the face, knocking him flat on his back.

When a few bystanders protested that Johnny had gone too far, the lanky deputy agreed. "You are right," he said. Then he marched down the hallway to the office of the justice of the peace. There he filed a case of simple assault against himself, pled guilty to the charge, was fined five dollars, pulled the appropriate bill out of his pocket and handed it to a surprised justice, and went back to his politicking sans the kibitzer. It would not be the last time he paid such a fine. All in all, it was not an untypical Bexar County election campaign.

Deputy Klevenhagen was not a complainer, but he was dedicated to his job and was not afraid to speak out when parsimonious politicians impeded the progress of law enforcement. After pointing out to county commissioners how Buster Kern's two tear gas grenades brought an end to the Red River Raider, Lawrence Rea, he asked for an appropriation to purchase eight tear gas grenades for the sheriff's office.

When an officious commissioner blocked the request on the grounds that Bexar County law officers had done without them for years and so "didn't need newfangled gadgets now," Johnny blew his top. He pointed out that the sheriff's deputies had installed modern fingerprinting facilities and a photographic department at their own personal expense.

"Commissioner, I can't understand your attitude," he said. "If you are opposed to newfangled things, why don't you use mules instead of a tractor when you are building county roads? And why don't you come to the courthouse in a horse and buggy instead of a Packard automobile?"

The commissioner only snorted. Things, however, would begin looking up. Soon afterward, Bexar County District Attorney Lawrence Shook hired Klevenhagen as his chief criminal investigator at a higher salary. It was helpful since John Jr. had made his appearance in the Klevenhagen household and was romping around with a deputy's badge pinned to his diaper. Families, Johnny Sr. learned, were not inexpensive.

Johnny was in his office at the Bexar County courthouse one August morning in 1941 when the telephone rang. Calling was Colonel Homer Garrison, director of the Texas Department of Public Safety, which included the overall supervision of the Texas Rangers. Garrison was a six-foot two, burly lawman who had rejuvenated the Ranger force after several decades of political patronage and interference, skimpy budgets, and overall low esteem had damaged the organization.

"Well, Johnny, you've been appointed a Texas Ranger," Garrison announced, "How do you like your new job?" Johnny let out a loud hurrah that echoed throughout the courthouse corridors. It had finally come, after more than a decade of waiting and hoping. He immediately telephoned Viola. "I'm a Ranger," he shouted, "Assigned to Houston. Start packing. I'll be sworn in at Austin, then we'll head for Houston."

He dashed into District Attorney Shook's office. "I've got to leave, Chief," he said, "I'm going to be a Ranger. Thanks for everything."

The D.A., sorry to lose his best investigator but happy for Johnny, gave a parting admonition as the new Ranger bolted out the door. "Shave off that damned mustache," he shouted after him, "Rangers don't wear mustaches."

It was good advice. Texas Rangers were expected to be neat, clean, and, depending on the job and the weather, were expected to wear a clean shirt, tie, and coat. Flamboyance in dress was not only frowned upon, it was a cause for a chewing out by Col. Garrison. On one occasion a newly appointed ranger arrived at the colonel's office for his swearing-in ceremony dressed in a multicolored embroidered cowboy shirt, skin-tight britches, a garish pair of cowboy boots of assorted leathers, and with a six-gun strapped low on each thigh.

Garrison took one look, rolled his eyeballs back in an appeal to heaven, then stared at the Roy Rogers look-alike and snarled, "Come back when you are wearing a decent suit of clothes or get a job in the movies."

It was difficult to become a Texas Ranger in those days, as it is today. There are always many more applicants for the job than there are vacancies on the force. In Johnny's time, a three-man board selected candidates who were more than twenty-eight years of age with at least seven years experience as a lawman. The candidate had to have a spotless reputation, proven courage, and an outstanding record as an investigator, and finally, be vetted by Col. Garrison.

On the morning of August 14, in Homer Garrison's office, Johnny took the oath of office. Although shorn of his dapper mustache and having taken a heavy cut in salary, he was an exceedingly happy man. The financial sacrifice was real. Starting out in the rangers as a criminal investigator, he received the magnificent sum of $175 per month; low even for pre-Pearl Harbor 1941.

After Johnny was sworn in and the ranger badge was pinned on a proud chest, Garrison gave him a few words of advice. It is tradition, Garrison said, that enables the rangers to wield an influence far out of proportion to their numbers. He stated, "Once a Ranger commits himself, he must not back down. If he is unable to master the situations he often finds himself in, he is expected to turn in his badge and avoid the added disgrace of having it taken away from him. This may seem a harsh policy but the effectiveness of the Rangers depends on it.

"The Ranger tradition to keep on coming is the most powerful weapon the Ranger has. It is far more powerful than his pistol. An armed mob can rush a Ranger, but every man in that mob knows that several people are going to get killed in the process. And one of them might be him. A man who falters at the critical moment, or who can't enforce his commands, destroys the Rangers' effectiveness. We can't have such men in the organization and we don't.

"Every man in the Rangers is a rugged individualist. You have to be because sometimes you will work alone. I don't give Rangers orders on an individual case because some of them are very touchy, besides our men know what they are doing. That's why they are Rangers."

"But," he implored, "try to make out decent reports." He quoted one old Ranger's documentation on the disposition of a case, which in its entirety read, "Fugitive was mean as the devil. Had to shoot him." "You must do better than that," Garrison stated.

It was the one piece of the colonel's advice that most rangers demonstrated a laxity in following.

Assigned to Ranger Company A, headquartered in Houston, Klevenhagen was under the command of Captain Hardy Purvis, a tough gamecock of a man who walked with a limp after being shot in the leg during one of his many gunfights. Purvis pointed out the awesome responsibilities of Company A, which held jurisdiction of forty-six southeast Texas counties.

Rangers are expected to work sixty to seventy hours a week, plunge into the most complicated and dangerous situations in the state, solve crimes and give most of the credit to local law officers, and freely risk their lives on any necessary occasion. In addition to the rough and tumble of police work with dangerous and desperate men, a ranger must also become a trained expert in fingerprinting, ballistics, state law, and in courtroom procedures. He must also be a diplomat in his dealings with local police chiefs and sheriffs. He would also be entitled to wear the famed ranger badge hammered out of a Mexican silver peso.

The forty-five-man ranger force, spread out over a state larger than most countries, was called in to help local law enforcement officers solve difficult crimes, because in 1941 many small towns and rural areas had inadequately trained police officers not conversant with either legal procedures or forensic evidence. When on the road, they were allowed the lucrative sum of six dollars per day for expenses.

In addition to being troubleshooters they also had the responsibility to help track down escaped convicts from Texas's penal institutions. At first, but later changed, they were required to use their own automobiles with a less than exorbitant mileage allowance. They also needed a good saddle for many chases and investigations that were held in off-the-road rough rural areas. And like rangers of a previous century they still did much of their work on horseback.

The trunk compartment of a ranger's automobile was a congested mess of rifles, cameras, plaster for making casts of foot or tire prints, shotguns, fingerprint sets, saddles, harnesses, and spurs. Most rangers, like Johnny, dressed ready for anything, wearing cowboy boots, Stetsons, and western-style suits. Their constant companion, off duty or on, was a .45-caliber Colt automatic pistol usually stuck in the waistband of their trousers. Johnny stuffed his in his belt, carried on half cock.

He had been a ranger only a few months when, returning to Houston from an investigation in East Texas, he received an all-points radio call reporting that an escaped felon from Eastham Prison was loose in his vicinity. The man had stolen a vehicle in Lovelady, run through a police roadblock, and was heading west on a country road.

Johnny, accompanied by a state highway patrolman, was driving near a Trinity River bridge when he spotted the stolen car heading toward him at a high rate of speed. He maneuvered his old Ford to block the roadway, but the convict swerved to one side, narrowly missing the Ford, and sped away. Johnny gunned his auto and they roared off in pursuit.

As both autos careened wildly down the narrow country road, the trooper leaned out of the right side window of the auto and opened fire with his .38-caliber revolver with no apparent result.

Johnny rolled down his window and with his right hand on the steering wheel, pulled his .45 automatic with his left. Leaning out the window, he opened fire from his weaving auto. He had emptied the magazine of his weapon when the stolen car began to veer to one side of the road, came to a screeching halt, and burst into flames.

The convict leaped from the flaming vehicle and ran limping toward the two officers who had stopped their car and stood waiting in the road. Holding one hand high in the air and the other clutching his posterior, he shouted, "Don't shoot. Don't shoot. Please don't shoot. I'm hit."

As the patrolman cuffed the convict, Johnny inspected him from the rear. There was a jagged rent in the man's pants and a deep crimson, blistered gouge across his buttock. As they were heading back to Eastham Prison in Johnny's car, the convict, cuffed in the backseat, trying to shift his weight off his aching bun, plaintively asked, "I got hit and the car practically blew up. What the hell were you shooting?"

Johnny grinned, "Tracers," he said.

A few months later the Empire of Japan, in one of the most gross stupidities in modern history, attacked the United States naval base at Pearl Harbor.

Johnny, who by now was a veteran pilot in the light airplane owned by the state of Texas, believed his flying skill would be of value to the Army Air Force. He drove to Randolph Field, an air corps base near San Antonio, and volunteered his services as a pilot. Desperate for experienced aviators and perhaps misunderstanding his flying experience, Air Corps officers allowed him to make a demonstration of his flying ability in a Curtiss P-40 "Tomahawk."

The officers were unaware that Johnny's experience as a pilot was limited to flying a fifty-horsepower Aeronica, which cruised at ninety miles per hour. At that time the Tomahawk was one of the fastest fighter planes in the Army Air Corps. Unused to the high-powered engine and the speed of the fighter, Johnny got it off the ground, but it was soon out of control. The Texas Ranger performed some inadvertent spins, banks, and aerobatics probably never seen since the days of the Red Baron.

Luckily, if not skillfully, Johnny finally got control of the aircraft and managed to land it with both he and the Tomahawk in one piece. It was a scary thirty minutes in the air, if not for Johnny, at least for the aghast Air Corps officers who had put a light plane pilot into the cockpit of a speedy fighter plane. Fortunately, perhaps for the Army Air Corps as well as for Johnny, he was "frozen" in his job as a Texas Ranger for the duration of the war.

In early 1942 a tall, rangy, broad shouldered, newly appointed ranger named Eddie Oliver joined Company A. Soft spoken, he was unlike other rangers in that he favored conservative business suits rather than the western garb most wore. He turned out to be smart, industrious, and tough, and he and Johnny were to work many dangerous and difficult cases together.

During the war years the rangers took on the additional duties of rounding up German aliens, working with local police in devising plans for protecting war plants and vital areas such as power plants, refineries, dams, and bridges.

They also helped track down the few German military prisoners who escaped from prisoner of war camps in Texas.

On February 22, 1942, Klevenhagen and other Rangers of Company A arrested seventy-seven German aliens residing in Houston. On February 27, accompanied by FBI agents, they raided seventy-two locations in Galveston, arrested forty-four German aliens, and confiscated all firearms and shortwave radios found in their houses. A number of Germans were placed in detention camps in Seagoville, Crystal City, and Kenedy, Texas.

Amusingly, the fighting valor of Texas Rangers, known around the world, created considerable confusion in the ranks of the Vichy French. On August 19, 1942, announcing the Allied raid on the French port of Dieppe, the French press reported the raiders consisted of British and Canadian commandos and a contingent of Texas Rangers. The French later explained they had confused U.S. Army Rangers with the Texas variety.

In early June 1943 Company A received word that two convicts had escaped from Ramsey Prison and made their way to Houston. One of the men, Joe McCamey, was a convicted murderer who boasted he would never be taken alive. The information was that the convicts had dumped their prison garb, acquired new clothing, and had armed themselves with pistols.

On a tip from one of his informants, Johnny located one of the men in a run-down rooming house near downtown Houston. After he was arrested and put under an intense interrogation, the man finally told police he was to rendezvous with McCamey at six o'clock that evening at a downtown street corner. At the appointed time Johnny and Oliver eased up to the meeting place. Just as they spotted McCamey, he spotted them.

As the two rangers ran toward the convict, a city bus pulled up and stopped and a stream of men, women, and small children spilled out on the sidewalk. Jumping into the midst of this crowd, McCamey pulled out a pistol and started shooting at the rangers at a distance of thirty feet. The lawmen, guns drawn, could not return fire for fear of hitting someone in the now panicked crowd.

McCamey, rattled, fortunately was a poor marksman. After firing seven times at the unflinching rangers, he managed to buzz one past Klevenhagen's ear, pierce the right sleeve of Oliver's coat, shoot out the windshield of a passing automobile, and blow out the tire of another.

"I couldn't shoot back," Johnny said, "And I damned sure couldn't run, so I hollered to that paralyzed bus driver to get his so-and-so bus out of there." The driver finally recovered his senses and drove off. The screaming crowd by this time had run down the street, giving Johnny a clear shot. He fired once and his heavy .45 slug hit the sleeve of the gunman's coat and jarred the pistol out of his hand.

"Let's get him," Johnny yelled, and he and Oliver made simultaneous running tackles that brought McCamey down.

In his laconic report to Captain Purvis, Johnny wrote, "Shot him loose from his pistol." When a newspaper reporter later asked Klevenhagen why he didn't blow McCamey away when the crowd cleared, he replied: "A star is no license to kill. An officer should never be proud of being tagged a gunfighter. No officer should ever kill another man unless he's forced. You should only shoot after the criminal has fired on you." It was a principle he always adhered to, and on more than one occasion it nearly cost him his life.

CHAPTER 6

The Beaumont Riots

Beaumont, Texas had been a sleepy, languid port on the Gulf of Mexico, shipping agricultural products and beef until the nearby Spindletop oil discovery in 1901 turned it into a roaring boomtown. As the city filled with wildcatters, roughnecks, land agents, and tool handlers, it also brought in the card sharks, con artists, prostitutes, and career criminals who came in to claim their share of black gold.

As oil gushed from the hundreds of wells in the area, crime and general hell raising created so much havoc that Texas Rangers were called in to calm down the rough, tough population. The industrial boom continued more quietly until the beginning of World War II. Then the city underwent another massive boom as war industries burgeoned along the Gulf Coast.

People from all over Texas and Louisiana, male and female, surged into the area to meet the demand for workers in war-related industries. One of the largest employers was the Philadelphia Shipworks, which employed thousands of workers building ships for the expanding merchant marine and navy.

In June 1943 the hot, steamy climate, where humidity covered one like a hot blanket, was even more irritating than usual with overcrowded housing, eateries, public buildings, and workplaces. Beaumont was also more of a Southern city than most of Texas, and relations between whites and blacks were less than cordial among many of the shipyard workers.

Added to the friction were the past legacy of boomtown violence and an East Texas heritage of an individual's reliance upon himself rather than legal authority in resolving personal injury or insult.

It all added up to an explosive social mix, and the fuse was lit on June 6. On that night a young white woman was returning from her job late in the evening when she was criminally assaulted by a black man in downtown Beaumont. When word of the attack spread, the latent hostility flared. The attacker was quickly cornered by police and shot to death. That quieted things down, but only temporarily.

Ten days later on the afternoon of Tuesday, June 16, a white mother of three was alone in her home on the west side of town while her husband worked at a war plant. She frantically telephoned police saying she had been criminally assaulted by a black man who had been wandering around her neighborhood. While the Beaumont police launched a prompt investigation, word of the attack spread like wildfire throughout the city.

When the tale of a black man raping a white mother spread through the Philadelphia shipyard, an estimated 5,000 workers dropped their tools and marched to the city jail and police station. Rumor had it that the black man responsible for the attack had been arrested and was being held in jail. As the furious men reached police headquarters, Judge Lynch was in the saddle and ready to ride.

Beaumont Detective Captain B.O. Craft reported, "They flooded in and took over the police station. We told them we had not arrested the accused rapist and were still looking for him." Unconvinced, the mob was about to seize and lynch four black men who had been arrested the previous night for shooting craps. As a last resort, the distraught mother was brought before the mob and told them she had looked at all the jail prisoners and none of them was the guilty party. The mob reluctantly left the jail and proceeded to charge into the black residential section of town.

At the first outbreak the Beaumont police and sheriff's office had alerted Governor Coke Stevenson that they could not control the raging mob. Stevenson immediately called out the Texas State Guard, a collection of volunteer citizens who took the place of the state's National Guard units, which were now overseas on the fighting fronts.

While the guard was mobilizing, Captain Purvis, Klevenhagen, and Oliver were burning up the highway on the ninety-mile drive from Houston to Beaumont. Arriving there, they aided police and sheriff's deputies in using tear gas grenades to disperse milling groups of angry white men.

An emergency call for help from the local bus station was relayed to the rangers, and Johnny and Oliver rushed to the depot while Captain Purvis organized a posse to search for the accused rapist, who was said to be hiding in a nearby wooded area.

Arriving at the beleaguered bus depot, Oliver later reported that a mob was outside the terminal trying to force open the locked doors. Their objective was a group of black draftees awaiting transportation to an Army induction center. Oliver said that the two rangers realized they could get no help from local police, who were still trying to clear the besieged police station.

But after all, the great legend of the Texas Rangers had always been, "One riot; one Ranger," and there were two of them. Parking at the edge of the mob, the two lawmen got out of their automobile, and Johnny unlocked the trunk compartment. "Grab a rifle," he said. Thus armed, the two rangers shouldered their way through the mob, and in front of the terminal they confronted the riot leaders.

"Get on home, all of you," Johnny shouted. When two of the leaders screamed defiance and moved on the lawmen, Oliver reported, "Johnny knocked one to the ground with his rifle barrel, and I cracked the other one upside the head."

Cuffing the two, Johnny announced, "These two are under arrest. The rest of you go home." With their leaders still groggy, the rest of the mob looked at the two tough rangers standing shoulder to shoulder and pointing rifles at their hearts. Mumbling and disgruntled, the men shuffled off. Most of them, however, did not return home but joined other gangs who throughout the evening dragged dozens of blacks from their autos and beat them.

All afternoon and early evening roving bands looted and burned more than a hundred homes. Johnny, the rest of the rangers, and other local officers sped from one place to another, arresting mob leaders and breaking up groups with tear gas and an occasional knock "alongside the head" of rowdy toughs.

By nightfall more than two thousand men of the 18th Battalion of the Texas State Guard arrived in town and assembled on the grounds of Beaumont High School. The next morning they completed the job of restoring order after a night of hysteria and terror. While the Guardsmen spread out, blocking streets and controlling intersections, the rangers and local lawmen made more than a hundred arrests.

When the city jail overflowed, officials roped off an area of the Jefferson County Fairgrounds to hold the prisoners. Highways were blocked, a "be off the streets by 8:30 P.M. or be arrested or shot" curfew was established. Busses were ordered to stop running, businesses were closed, and residents were told to stay indoors until morning.

By Wednesday evening order was restored to the city. The *Houston Post* newspaper reported, "Beaumont went to sleep Wednesday night under a blanket of guns."

Thursday was hangover quiet. Over the raucous twenty-four hours, two men had been killed. A black man, John Johnson, was dragged from his automobile and shot to death. A white man, Ellis Brown, after an affray, was found dead with a fractured skull. Scores were treated at the local hospital, over a dozen were seriously injured. A hundred houses had been looted and burned. Several automobiles in black neighborhoods had been burned and a score of stores looted. Four separate shooting scrapes were reported. And more than a day's worth of war production had been wasted.

The population of 150,000, of which 45,000 were black, was polarized for months, and hate simmered just below the surface. The "Juneteenth" celebration scheduled for June 19, which observed the liberation of blacks from slavery in the state of Texas, was banned as too inflammatory. All of those arrested were later turned loose. The black man who attacked the white woman was never found. Beaumont paid a high price for its twenty-four hours of racial frenzy.

A few months later Johnny and Oliver were summoned back to Beaumont at the outbreak of labor unrest. Harris County Chief Deputy Lloyd Frazier reported that when the two arrived at the disputed refinery, they found "some 400 people congregating to wreck a petroleum plant. They were being urged to violence by some fellow standing on a box."

According to Frazier, Johnny grabbed the firebrand orator by the ankle and jerked him to the ground. Then Johnny climbed onto the box and in a roaring voice told the assembled mob that if there was any violence to be done, "The Rangers will do it." The crowd took one long look at the two tall rangers, decided the satisfaction of arson and mayhem were not worth the risk of certain death, and then meekly turned and left the area.

In later times a story was told in newspaper reporters' press rooms in Houston that Johnny was summoned to the Houston docks one morning. There was, it was said, a jurisdictional dispute between the longshoremen and the teamsters unions that threatened to break into violence.

When Johnny arrived on the scene, a large congregation of husky dock-wallopers and truck drivers were standing face to face hollering insults at each other. Violence was just about to break out.

Johnny got out of his automobile carrying a folding chair in one hand and a twelve-gauge shotgun in the other. "All you fellas pay attention," he shouted. He unfolded the chair and leaned it up against the side of a warehouse on the wharf. He took a piece of chalk out of his pocket and leaning over, traced a line across the middle of the dock area separating the two groups. "Now," he said, "you teamsters stay on this side of the line and you longshoremen stay on the other side."

Johnny walked back to the chair, sat down, tipped the chair back to the wall, and stretched out. He positioned the shotgun across his lap, shifted the .45 at his belt, and announced, "The first bunch that tries to cross the line won't make it." Then he tilted his Stetson over his eyes against the glaring Gulf Coast sun and warily watched while the tough union men meekly drifted away. None wanted to bet his life that Johnny wouldn't use the shotgun or the .45.

The story was never confirmed. Maybe it was just one more tale in the growing legend of Johnny Klevenhagen. Maybe it wasn't.

During the war years, Ranger Klevenhagen told newspaper reporter Stan Redding that he estimated he averaged seventy-hour work weeks. He worked 974 criminal cases in 62 counties including 7 bank robberies, 144 murders, 349 burglaries, 3 kidnappings, and 109 armed robberies plus hunting down escaped prisoners and other sundry felonies.

It took a terrible toll on the all-too-conscientious Ranger. In 1946 he suffered a severe case of ulcers brought on by too many hours on the job, a poor diet often consisting of coffee and cigarettes, nervous strain, and lack of proper sleep. According to his wife, Viola, "The operation removed three quarters of his stomach. He worked too hard. During a case he never rested or ate properly, and all he did was gulp black coffee and smoke cigarettes."

As a result of the operation, Viola said it was difficult for him to regain his normal weight. From a lean, tough, muscular frame, Johnny looked more gaunt. There were circles beginning under his eyes and new lines on his face. It was the beginning of the physical sacrifices he would make in his dedication to the Ranger service.

CHAPTER 7

The Late Giacona

In the latter part of August 1945, the greatest war in history had ended and the men were coming home. But in Houston, in the ongoing battle against criminals, there was no light at the end of the tunnel.

On the humid, sweaty night of August 23, Klevenhagen, Sheriff Buster Kern, and Houston detective J.D. Walters were patrolling down a Houston street near the waterfront when they saw two shadowy figures slip into a dark alley behind a large department store. Walters said, "One of those guys looks like Sam Giacona, and he's probably after a safe." Giacona was a persistent if not a clever safecracker who was better known for his viciousness than his ability as a thief.

He was not one of those professionals who with a stethoscope and sandpapered fingers could hear the tumblers click and then deftly open most store safes. Giacona was a knocker, one who takes a sledgehammer to the combination dial and smashes it in and if that doesn't work, uses a crowbar and a sledge to peel back and smash open the safe door.

One member of the Houston police burglary detail looking at the huge mess of a safe smashed to smithereens by Giacona was heard to remark, "I wish he'd use nitro instead of a sledge." When another detective demurred, "Giacona's so dumb, he'd blow himself up." "Exactly," replied the first detective.

The thirty-six-year-old criminal had been a thorn in the side of the Houston police since he was first arrested as a teenager in 1927. He had a rap sheet showing more than fifty arrests and had been convicted of felonies and sent to state prison on three different occasions. In the few months since he had been released in the spring of 1945, Giacona had been arrested seven times and then released for lack of evidence. In those days a notorious convict, sighted in suspicious circumstances, could be arrested and held on an open charge of suspicion for twenty-four hours. If no evidence of a crime was forthcoming, he was released. In recent years, however, the United States Supreme Court, with dubious wisdom, considered such arrests as harassment and therefore illegal, thus giving another break to the criminal class.

In his latest arrest Giacona was picked up loitering near a loan company at closing time. As he was being released after questioning by police, he turned toward the detectives and snarled, "I wasn't doing anything illegal. If you guys come at me again, you better come shooting." Then he swaggered out into the street. It was a threat the lawmen took seriously.

That August night when Giacona was spotted, Kern drove the sheriff's car around the block, cut off the lights, killed the engine, and coasted into the alley in the rear of the department store. The three lawmen sat quietly in the car and all was still for a few minutes. Then they heard a muffled pounding coming from the office in the rear of the building. "He's knocking the safe," Johnny grinned.

Kern said, "Let's get him." The three piled out of the car and Johnny said, "Buster, you take the front door and Walters you take the rear. I'm going up on the roof and through the skylight. Give me a couple of minutes before you move in." Then the three men slipped out into the darkness.

Klevenhagen walked to the end of the alley, found a sturdy drainpipe that led all the way up to the roof, tilted his Stetson to the back of his head, and pulled himself up, hand over hand, with his cowboy boots digging into the pipe as if it were the flanks of a mean horse. Reaching the roof, he pulled himself onto the tarred surface and tiptoed over to an open skylight.

Leaning through the open hatch, Johnny turned on his flashlight and swept the office below only to hear a string of curses as the two surprised safecrackers were illuminated in the act of tearing up the store safe. Blinking at the light, Giacona was holding a sledgehammer and his companion, nineteen-year-old Donald Hutchinson, was inserting a crowbar in the space between the safe wall and the safe door. As Klevenhagen yelled, "Hands up," the two, momentarily frozen by the light beam, reacted and ran out of the office and down an aisle toward the back door of the store.

As the two burglars forced open the back door, they met Walters coming in. As Giacona leaped backward, Walters yelled, "Drop it," to Hutchinson who lunged forward, still gripping the crowbar. In the darkness Walters thought he was holding a pistol, and he squeezed the trigger on his twelve-gauge shotgun. The blast struck the teenager in the right leg. With blood spurting from his almost severed limb, Hutchinson fell backwards and writhed in a growing pool of blood while Giacona turned and ran back to the office.

There he picked up the automatic pistol he had laid down as he had started pounding the safe door. As Walters shot, Johnny was lowering himself from the skylight, when his flashlight shined upon the ugly, contorted face of Giacona. When the burglar raised his pistol, Johnny yelled, "Drop it and surrender." His answer was a curse, and Johnny, momentarily helpless, half suspended in the air, one hand grasping the edge of the skylight and the other holding the flashlight, thought his luck had run out as he saw Giacona cock the hammer of his automatic pistol.

But then Walters burst into the room and again fired his riot gun with deadly accuracy. A full load of double aught buckshot struck Giacona in the side, blowing a hole through his innards the size of a grapefruit. The burglar sprawled backwards into a pile of shoeboxes. Shoes and parts of Giacona scattered into and mixed with the cement packing of the safe door on the floor of the office.

Sending out a call for an ambulance for Hutchinson, Walters lamented, "I'm sorry I had to shoot the kid. I recognize him now. He's just a dumb junkie we've arrested for possession a dozen times."

Klevenhagen replied, "Don't worry about it. He called the tune, he has to pay the piper. Besides, he'll live." And Hutchinson did survive for a long time in the state penitentiary, but minus his right leg, which surgeons were forced to amputate.

Giacona netted only ten dollars, all that was in the safe he smashed, plus a plot in potter's field. Part of the ten-dollar loot was a silver dollar. Johnny pulled out his wallet, tossed a dollar bill on the floor, and pocketed the silver coin. For luck, he gave it to one of the old convicts he had befriended, who pounded it flat, welded a piece of metal to the back of it, thus fashioning a rather stylish money clip. Johnny carried it for years as a reminder that cracking safes and pointing a gun at a Texas Ranger is a form of crime that never pays.

As Klevenhagen's exploits became more widely known, one citizen, not quite tongue in cheek, wrote the *Houston Chronicle* newspaper advising that he had sent a telegram to President Eisenhower suggesting if the Soviets invaded the United States and advanced on Texas, "Just send Johnny Klevenhagen and two other Texas Rangers and they will drive them all into the Red River." Over a period of time other similar letters were sent to newspapers. A consensus was that the authors only exaggerated slightly.

CHAPTER 8

The Brute's Last Mistake

There is a saying among Texas criminals that "You can see a graveyard in the end of a Texas Ranger's gun." Even bad men of minimum intelligence know better than to take on a ranger in a gun battle. It's a lose-lose proposition. Still, there are always a few too foolish or too reckless to heed the saying. The late Rufe Lucas was such a fool.

Lucas was a cross-country truck driver who used his vagabond travels as a cover for his real life's work which was to rob, rape, and kill.

In late 1945 he struck in San Antonio, raping, robbing, and beating an unfortunate woman to death. Both brutal and stupid, he left behind enough clues to get police on his trail almost immediately.

One evening a few days after the murder, a Galveston police officer spotted the brute sitting in a café calmly drinking a cup of coffee. The officer entered the café, with his service revolver holstered, and told Lucas he was under arrest. Lucas smiled, affably paid his bill, and unresisting was led out to the officer's parked patrol car. The lawman, however, made an almost fatal mistake. He failed to hand-cuff the burly trucker.

As Lucas ducked his head to enter the auto, he suddenly spun around and lunged at the officer, smashing him into the car door. While the policeman was momentarily stunned, Lucas reached down and pulled the officer's service revolver from his holster. Clutching the weapon, he struck the officer again and ran down an alley, escaping into the darkness. Recovering, the chagrined officer immediately radioed police headquarters, and soon most of the force began an intensive manhunt.

In those days there were only four ways for a fugitive to get on or get off the island of Galveston. One could swim with the jellyfish and the pollution of Galveston Bay, steal a boat, hop a freight car and ride the rails across the railroad causeway, or, most likely, drive across the two-mile automobile causeway that connects the island with the mainland.

Within minutes the Galveston police force had all four avenues well covered. Alerted to the spreading manhunt, Johnny made a fast fifty-mile drive from his home to the island in time to join the posse.

Late that evening two Galveston policemen spotted Lucas driving a stolen car and took up the pursuit. There followed a wild police chase down Broadway, the main street leading to the causeway, with Lucas steering with one hand while clutching a pistol and shooting back at the police car with the other. Tourists and local motorists scrambled to get out of the way.

More than a dozen police cars, including Johnny's, summoned by radio, soon got on the tail of the fleeing killer and began to box him in. Lucas swerved from the main thoroughfare into a side road and drove into a run-down section of town. At one of the darkened intersections he suddenly braked, leapt out of the auto, and ran down an alley, losing himself in the night.

When police dashed to the stolen auto, they found the owner lying on the floorboards in a pool of blood. Lucas had earlier acquired his ride by approaching a stopped automobile, shooting the driver, shoving him down on the floor of the car, and driving away.

As a score of officers surrounded the area and began searching, Johnny spotted muddy footprints leading to what was locally known as a "shotgun house." This is a narrow wooden building resting on cinder blocks. The term comes from the theory that firing a shotgun through the front doorway would blow everything in the house out the back door.

The lawmen set up a cordon around the house as Johnny tracked the footprints to the side of the building. Rifle in hand, Johnny walked up to the house and shouted, "Come out of there, Lucas. Throw your gun out first and you won't be hurt."

Lucas hollered back, "I surrender. Don't shoot." The man, in a frantic effort to hide, had crawled underneath the building and lay huddled behind one of the cinder blocks. Again shouting, "I surrender. Don't shoot," he threw the police officer's stolen revolver out from under the house.

Johnny stooped to pick up the weapon, tucked it in his belt, and, cradling his .30-caliber carbine, shouted, "OK, come out."

Whether it was a crazed hatred for lawmen or a desire to commit "suicide by cop" (where a felon lacking the willpower to take his own life forces police to kill him) will never be known. But after he crawled out from under the house, Lucas stood up as if to brush the dirt from his clothes and pulled a .44-caliber Colt revolver out from his shirt.

A police officer named Campbell yelled, "Look out, Johnny," and drew his holstered pistol.

Johnny twisted to his left as a bullet buzzed close by and with his rifle on his hip squeezed off a shot as Campbell and police officer Alec Wier also quickly fired at Lucas. All three police bullets struck their mark and Lucas fell backwards. He was probably dead before his body hit the ground.

Campbell's .38-caliber bullet struck him in the chest, Wier's shot from his .45 ripped his stomach, and Johnny's missile fired from his Remington rifle blew out the brute's heart.

When one of the officers asked, "Are you hit?" Johnny fingered a newly made bullet hole in the sleeve of his jacket and shrugged, "He missed me."

It wasn't the only time a criminal bullet missed the ranger's lean body, and soon superstitious members of the underworld spread the word that Johnny Klevenhagen was immune to bullets.

One former gunman serving a long prison term in Huntsville Penitentiary told *Houston Chronicle* reporter Stan Redding, "When he came to arrest me, I pulled my gun and pointed it at him. But he never slowed down and kept coming. I could see his eyes burning into me, and I could see death in them. He told me to either shoot or drop the gun. I dropped the gun. If I hadn't, somehow I knew he would kill me." Another convict once said, "Johnny don't always shoot fast, but he damn well shoots straight."

Texas Rangers were more than just straight shooters when it came to firearms. The philosophy of the force was always to keep a low profile, and grandstanders were held in low regard.

Johnny, like all Texas Rangers, and with good reason, believed the rangers were the premiere law enforcement organization on the planet Earth. And like the rest of the rangers, he practiced giving most of the credit for solved cases to the local police or sheriff's department. There was a certain antipathy toward other organizations that often claimed undeserved credit for the work of others and often muscled themselves into a solved case.

There was one widely heralded incident when an FBI agent walked into Johnny's office unannounced. As he entered the room the FBI agent stated, "I'm going to ask you some questions."

Leaning back in his chair, Johnny propped his high-heeled boots upon his desk, gave the agent a long, hard stare, tipped his Stetson back, and replied, "Sonny, I don't answer questions; I ask them." Then with his index finger he pointed to the door. After a moment of utter silence, the FBI agent quietly left the office. It was an incident that was told and retold with much amusement by Houston police officers and Harris County sheriff's deputies.

CHAPTER 9

Murder, Gangland Style

At the end of World War II, Houston, Texas resembled a bright, brawling adolescent boy. Sure of his brawny muscular strength, exuberant in his newfound potency, albeit with a lingering doubt about his not yet emerged sophistication, but charged with a blustering desire to prove himself, bigger, better, richer, and tougher than anyone else.

As the Marshall Plan began reviving a prostrate Europe, wheat, soybeans, corn, and other cereal grains from the Great Plains states and the Middle West flowed south, joining the rice, cotton, and citrus of Texas in a mighty stream that culminated at the docks of the Port of Houston. There, loaded on freighters, these life-giving cargoes wended their way through the fifty-mile-long ship channel to the Gulf of Mexico and then northeastward to Europe.

Lining the ship channel were massive petrochemical complexes and petroleum refineries that were newly built or under construction. There were giant plants that chewed wood pulp and rags into paper, clanging steel mills hammering sheet metal into pipe, while floating oil rigs and gaunt steel barges regularly slid down wooden ways into the oil and chemical soaked water of the channel.

In downtown Houston multilane freeways were ripped through old neighborhoods as skyscrapers, first twenty, then thirty, then forty stories high, blotted out the sun and brought welcome shade to sidewalks and streets crammed with pedestrians and automobiles. To those who complained of the stink of chemicals, oil, and paper mills and the cacophony of stalled traffic and raging jackhammers that filled the air, local businessmen replied, "It is the smell and sound of gold."

At night the ship channel was lit by hundreds of bright orange flames leaping into the sky as oil and natural gas wells burned off their waste gases. From an airplane the flames resembled a giant torchlight parade marching out to sea.

At that time in Texas, the city police were in charge of criminal investigation within the city's limits, while the sheriff's department held jurisdiction throughout the rest of the county. The Texas Rangers moved into investigations only when invited by the local authorities or at the orders of the governor or the attorney general of the state. So it was in Houston, and the various policing authorities, each jealous of their jurisdictions and each responsible to a different set of elected officials, were very careful not to step on each other's booted toes.

Shortly after the war, Houston had what might, with charity, be called a laissez-faire attitude toward vice. There were several "protected" whorehouses in downtown Houston—one where the ladies paraded before clients dressed like Scarlett O'Hara in the Southern belle costumes featured in *Gone With the Wind*. Often, beer joints had marble tables, slot machines, and bartenders who would take a bet on a horse, a quarterback, or a pitcher.

Discharged from the army in 1946 and still in uniform, the author walked into a downtown lounge one mid-afternoon. Sipping a draft beer at the bar, I observed through a wide open door toward the rear of the lounge a craps table crowded with players. A croupier with gartered sleeves and a green eye shade droned out the roll of the dice while the players loudly groaned or cheered. The plaintive cries of "Gimme an eighter from Decatur," a "seven from heaven," or a cursed "snake eyes" rang through the lounge.

Suddenly the door to the street opened and a uniformed police officer strode in. Walking into the gambling room, he gave no cry of "Y'all are under arrest," but a shout, "Whoever owns that blue '47 Chrysler, you left your lights on." There followed a muttered oath and a "Thanks, Officer," as a sportily dressed man walked out into the street. The police officer leaned up against the bar as the bartender placed a glass of draft beer in front of him. This was Houston in 1946.

There were newly made multimillionaire oil wildcatters like Glen McCarthy, who often got fighting drunk and was thrown out of so many hotel ballrooms that he built his own hotel, the fabulous Shamrock, where he feted the high and low of Hollywood in its gaudy green ballrooms. Edna Ferber wrote a roman à clef fantasy about it and called it *Giant*. Hollywood made it into a movie starring Elizabeth Taylor, Rock Hudson, and James Dean at the height of their careers. When it was shown in local theaters, both the habitues of café society and beer joint philosophers panned it for understatement.

Compared to Houston, local boosters were fond of saying other boomtowns were pikers. All agreed Houston was a city ripe with promise. There were others, however, who believed it was a city ripe for plucking. And the Cosa Nostra was ready to pluck.

In Galveston the Maceos reigned supreme behind the Maceo-Dickinson Line, which referred to a small town just inside Galveston County. Within the line bars and restaurants had dice and card tables and slot machines and a wire service gave results from horse tracks across the country. Rumor had it the Maceos were "made" members of an Eastern Mafia family.

In Houston, however, gambling and vice were run by various local individuals. It was the one big city in which organized crime had not gained a foothold. One of the biggest gamblers was said to be Vincent Vallone, a restaurant owner and the operator of the biggest horse racing bookie business in town. In the 1930s Vallone had worked for the Maceos as the manager of the High-Hat Club, a nightclub and gambling casino operating in Houston. But at this, Houston authorities balked. The rule of Houston vice to be run by Houstonians only was being violated. They ordered a bulky assistant district attorney named Percy Foreman to lead a raid that closed down the High-Hat and seized several thousand dollars' worth of gambling equipment in the process. The Maceos, rebuked, thereafter confined their activities behind the Line.

Vallone went out on his own. His Houston wire service was said to be a big moneymaker, and he was reputed to be planning to open a Galveston-style casino in Houston. Soon, it was rumored that the Mafia wanted a slice of this rich Texas pie. The Eastern bosses made Vallone an offer he couldn't refuse. But he did and he shouldn't have.

At 10 P.M. on the night of July 15, 1949, he was driving home alone in his Cadillac. He was only a few miles from his palatial mansion on Chocolate Bayou Road when a black sedan pulled up alongside. A man leaned out the rear window of the sedan, poked a twelve-gauge shotgun a few feet from the Cadillac's rear window, and squeezed the trigger. A load of double aught buckshot blasted through the window and blew out the back of Vallone's head. As he slumped over the front seat, a second blast missed the car and peppered a schoolteacher's house near the side of the road. That shot wasn't necessary; the first shot killed Vallone instantly. The Cadillac rolled to a stop, and a startled neighbor told police that the black sedan sped off into the night. When police found the body they noted a nice touch. There was a red rosebud, somewhat bloody, in the lapel of his expensive jacket. Vallone had once owned a nightclub called the Villa Rosa. His false teeth, blown out of his head by the shotgun blast, were found on the floor of the car.

The "Wise Men" in Houston were said to remark, "Vince should have known better than to buck the mob. He knew them. Hell, he was once one of them."

Vallone, who was sixty-five years old at his death, was born in Calabria, in southern Italy. He came to the United States when he was eighteen years old and originally settled in New York. But he soon came to Houston where he became a restaurateur, a gambler, and some said, a hit man for the Cosa Nostra.

In 1938 he and Sam Maceo were tried in a federal court on a charge of selling narcotics, but they both were acquitted. Later that year Vallone was involved in a barroom brawl during which time he pumped five bullets into one Sam Ferrugia. Vallone was charged with assault to murder but when Ferrugia amazingly recovered and fled the city, the police had to drop the charge. In 1941 he was convicted of murdering a railroad man after an argument, and the court gave him a ninety-nine-year prison sentence. After serving four years in prison, he was given a pardon in 1946 and released. In 1947 he opened the Villa Rosa and later an Italian restaurant named the Sorrento.

For years the police suspected him of being a trigger man for a Sicilian mob, and ironically his murder was in the best bravura tradition of that ignoble organization.

When it was first suggested that an imported assassin might have been the trigger man, a deputy sheriff debunked the idea saying, "Why should a killer have been imported when there are a jillion people around here who'd like to have killed him?" Indeed, there was no lack of suspects. Adding to the mystery was a telephone call to the *Houston Post*. A deep-voiced man told an editor, "Vallone's killers won't ever be convicted. They'll be taken care of the way he was....We know who did it. They came from Galveston....They are louses." The man further stated Vallone was killed by men who owed him money. Perhaps.

The murder, of course, had all the ingredients that make for a media feeding frenzy. The furor reunited the two most famous Houston lawmen, Texas Ranger John Klevenhagen and the newly elected Harris County Sheriff C.V. "Buster" Kern. In the past the two working together had cracked so many dangerous and difficult cases that a grateful press named them "The Gold Dust Twins" of law enforcement.

One of the reasons the two men worked so well together is that they not only resembled each other but came from similar backgrounds. They both had the lanky, lean, leathery look of men who were raised to outdoor hard work; and they shared a perceptive intelligence, dogged determination, and a very tough demeanor.

Kern was slender, strong as a wire rope, with a pursed mouth and a dangerous look. Slightly under six feet, he wore a snap brim fedora cocked over one eye and pulled down toward his nose. His steely blue eyes seemed to bore into a felon like an avenging Torquemada. Criminals often said they believed that if they lied to him, he would know it and would call down a lightning bolt to strike them dead.

Buster was born on a farm in rural Louisiana in 1904. The nickname came early and was a form of self-protection for a boy christened Clairville Vincent Kern. The family moved to Houston when Buster was seven years old. He quit school after the eighth grade and went to work at odd jobs to help with the family income.

When World War I broke out, the gangly fourteen-year-old convinced army recruiters he was eighteen. Hungry for fresh cannon fodder, they swore him into the enlisted ranks where he served for more than five months until they found out his true age and with a friendly pat on the back gave him a discharge with the request he try again in about four years.

A civilian again, Buster went back to unskilled laboring jobs until at age seventeen when he applied for a job as a Houston police officer. Perhaps hard work and hardship had aged him beyond his years, because like Klevenhagen, he convinced the department he was twenty-one years old. He was so tall and skinny, the department had to waive the weight requirement to get this hard-looking young man on the force.

He started out as a foot patrolman on the mean streets of Houston, but after a few months he graduated to patrolling on horseback. Then, also like Klevenhagen, he became a motorcycle officer. Highly intelligent and hardworking, he was promoted up the ranks until 1941 when he was appointed chief of detectives. It was then that he and the newly minted Texas Ranger Johnny Klevenhagen began their greatest collaboration. Soon their names became oaths to the underworld while they became legends to law enforcement officers throughout Texas.

Both were workaholics. Kern later said, "On a big murder case, I'd work four or five days straight with no time out except to change my socks." Klevenhagen mirrored the same dedication.

The Vallone murder left a tangled trail of false clues, suspects questioned then dropped, disappearing witnesses, and a myriad of rumors blaming everyone from the New York Cosa Nostra to the Detroit Purple Gang for the murder. In the midst of all this, a haggard Buster Kern campaigned and was elected sheriff of Harris County.

The case was broken wide open at 10 A.M. on October 15 when a thirty-one-year-old grocer named Diego Carlino was driving his produce truck en route to his store. Suddenly, a police car pulled ahead and swerved in front of him. Carlino slammed on his brakes, coming to a shuddering stop. Four police officers, Sheriff Kern, Ranger Klevenhagen, and two deputy sheriffs, leaped from their auto and, with drawn pistols, pulled Carlino from the truck and handcuffed him. To keep the Houston press and defense lawyers away until they could question him, they took Carlino to the nearby port city of Texas City and booked him in the city jail. From that point on there are two entirely different and conflicting stories about one of the most bizarre series of events in Texas criminal history.

Carlino, a dark-haired, blue-eyed, slightly built ex-paratrooper and alleged war hero, was a New Yorker who had come to Houston after his discharge from the army in 1945. There he opened and operated a grocery store until the time of his arrest. When his wife learned of his arrest, she hired Percy Foreman, the state's most flamboyant and controversial defense lawyer, to represent her husband. Then the fireworks began.

Percy Foreman was a six-foot-four-inch, 285-pound mixture of blubber, brains, babble, and bluster who probably enabled more murderers to escape justice than any other Texas criminal attorney. Although he represented more than a thousand accused killers during his career, only one was ever executed and that was because the murderer made the mistake of shooting his wife in the head while she was sitting on the toilet. It was probably the indelicacy of the killing that upset the jurors. More ominous was the fact that only fifty-five of those thousand killers ever served even a day in jail.

Stories about Percy abounded in the courts of the state, and probably the most outrageous were true. Percy was also good at defending himself and successfully beat the rap on various charges of adultery, subornation of perjury, operating a numbers racket, and using abusive language. He told a San Angelo newspaper reporter that in 1952 he defended twelve women who had killed their husbands and got "not guilty" verdicts in each case.

This bore out the oft-told anecdote that while at a cocktail party a wealthy woman said to Percy, "I want you to represent me. I want a divorce." Percy was said to reply, "Better to shoot him. It's cheaper."

Some said Percy just hated authority. Any authority. The author, while a Houston newspaper reporter, remembers when a band of gypsies were dragged before a magistrate's court charged with panhandling, petty theft, and gambling. Percy happened to pass by and a gypsy called out, "Percy, defend us." Foreman agreed, conferred with the gypsy "king," and approached the bench.

"Your Honor," he said, "My clients are not fluent in the English language and do not understand the charges against them. They speak and understand only the Romany tongue. To enable them to have a fair trial I request the court to provide a Romany translator before we proceed."

The magistrate glared at the bangled and spangled crew of ragamuffins before him, probably pondered the impossibility of finding anyone who could speak gypsy, turned to Percy and said, "Get yourself and this band of thieves the hell out of my court. Case dismissed."

When someone asked Percy if he was ashamed to keep so many criminals from punishment, he laughed saying, "They're plenty punished when they get my bill."

Bulky, jowly, with a lion's mane of long salt and pepper hair, Percy would hover over jurors oozing a good ol' boy charm. He would bellow like a bull as he tore into police officers and district attorney investigators on the witness stand, but he could be as sweet talking as a lingerie salesman when he was recounting the horrible injustices done to his virginal clients by the evil minions of the law.

He used what is now called the O.J. Simpson defense, but Percy had perfected it long before that football player was born. It was a simplistic recipe of defense. First you used your peremptory challenges (these enable an attorney to eliminate members of the jury panel without giving a reason) to get rid of the most educated and intelligent members of the jury panel. Then you try to weed out for cause anyone else who might possibly have the brains to go beyond rhetoric and analyze facts.

Sadly, the only qualifications for jury service in Texas are that one must be an American citizen, at least pretend to understand the English language, and have never been convicted of a felony. Because many steady middle-class and professional people have a propensity for finding excuses from serving, Texas juries are all too often composed of the less educated and less sophisticated citizens.

If a defense attorney was skilled enough, he often ended up with a jury who moved their lips when they read newspaper headlines.

The next rule was to never let the district attorney concentrate on trying your defendant. Attack. Never defend. The police, you claim, framed your client. They lied, were sympathetic to the Ku Klux Klan, were Nazis at heart. All confessions are the result of unspeakable tortures. The district attorney is a clumsy fool who bungled the evidence, or he is an ambitious politician willing to send your innocent client to the electric chair to further his own career. In extremis, you proved your client killed in self-defense and that the victim deserved to be deceased.

Unfortunately, slick, glib attorneys often confuse naive, under-educated jurors into verdicts that are perversions of justice. At this, Percy Foreman was the acknowledged master.

With Carlino in the dock, the two sides squared off. Evidence seemed to be irrelevant in the proceedings that followed, for the contest was between Kern and Klevenhagen representing law and order and Percy Foreman representing a fat fee. It would not be an edifying spectacle.

CHAPTER 10

Carlino on Trial

The judicial three-ring circus that was to last for two and a half years began after Carlino's arrest. When they took him into custody, they spirited him to the Texas City jail where they booked him for murder. Carlino claimed they secretly transferred him to a lonely hunting lodge deep in the piney woods of East Texas.

There, he said, they tied him to a wooden chair and "Two gorillas called Red and Harry beat me up. They punched me in the stomach so hard I was flung back and broke the chair. As I laid on the floor they poked me in the stomach."

While he was screaming with pain, Carlino said, Klevenhagen told him, "Go ahead and holler, there is no one to hear you except the hogs and the frogs." Then, Carlino said the ranger told him, "Talk or you won't leave here alive."

When he still refused to confess, Carlino said Red and Harry put a rope around his neck and strung him to a rafter and continued to beat him for three hours until he passed out.

On October 18 Carlino was brought to the Houston County jail and charged with murder. Sheriff Kern produced a long detailed confession signed by Carlino. When questioned by newspaper reporters, Carlino pleaded his innocence, "I signed something at Texas City, but I was groggy because of the terrible beating and I did not know what I was signing." When the author interviewed Carlino alone in his cell, he said, "Listen, I would have confessed to killing Cock Robin; I would have said I assassinated Abraham Lincoln if they would only stop hitting me."

Admitting there were no bruise marks either on his face or his stomach, Carlino maintained, "The men who beat me up were so smart and expert they didn't leave marks." Asked why there were no rope burns on his neck, Carlino reported, "They wrapped a cloth around the rope."

Not surprisingly, Klevenhagen and Kern told an entirely different story. Throughout, Kern, because of his political position, became the spokesman for the two. The sheriff denied Carlino was beaten or that he had been taken from the Texas City jail except to be transferred to Houston.

During interrogation, Kern reported that Carlino told them that Vallone summoned him to his office and asked him to kill a rival gambler named "Hunchback" Wolfe. According to Kern, Carlino stated, "I'm sorry I killed Vallone, but it was either kill him or be forced into killing someone else." The grocer said he threw the shotgun used in the killing into Buffalo Bayou. Then, according to Kern, Carlino took law officers to the Sabine River Bridge from where he had thrown the weapon.

The Sheriff's Department deployed a 3,000-pound electro magnet to the spot and combed the bottom of the bayou, but the shotgun was not found. Then, four young boys in the area told a policeman they saw a junk dealer pull a shotgun out of the bayou. Police rushed to the junkyard and retrieved a rusting shotgun. Since there is no rifling (lands and grooves) in the barrel of a shotgun and the pellets fired are not marked by the gun's smooth barrel, ballistic tests could not be used to determine if this was the weapon that killed Vallone.

On the basis of his confession and circumstantial evidence, Carlino was indicted by a Harris County grand jury on a charge of murder. A man named Louis J. Marino was charged as the driver of the death car the night Vallone was murdered, but he was never indicted by a grand jury and the charges were dropped. During October 1950 a mishmash of a trial was held in which both sides claimed they were handicapped by missing witnesses, and attorneys on both sides tried to outdo each other in vitriol. At the end of it, a confused jury reached an impasse and could not render a verdict. Carlino was freed on a $20,000 bond, and both prosecutors and defense attorneys girded for the next round.

It began on February 21, 1952, in the 51st District Court in San Angelo, Judge John F. Sutton presiding. Percy was again on hand for the defense. Relatives of Vallone hired a special prosecutor, who was aided by the San Angelo district attorney and an assistant district attorney from Houston.

After attorneys exchanged a few preliminary barbs and spectators laughed, the judge spoke to the court bailiff, saying, "If that happens again, remove them from the courtroom. If they return, put them in jail." Next, Judge Sutton levied $900 worth of fines on three witnesses who were not present when court opened.

After a jury had been selected, the no-nonsense judge, hearing rumors that some witnesses had been discussing the case with each other, called them in and threatened, "The county maintains a building across the street where two meals are served each day. If witnesses are talking among themselves or with anyone else, they will be put over there eating those two meals during this trial."

Judge Sutton was a stickler for punctuality. If witnesses were late, he told them, they would be fined two dollars per late minute. The judge could prevent a tardy court, but even he could not prevent the fireworks that followed.

Sheriff Kern, the first witness for the prosecution, testified that Carlino led Klevenhagen and him to the spot on Buffalo Bay where he dumped the murder weapon. He said Carlino told them he would take full blame for the killing because if he didn't, the Mafia would kill his wife, his mother, and his father. Carlino told the officers, according to Kern, that while a man named Louis Marino drove the car, he sat in the backseat from where he fired the fatal shots.

The next witness was a thirty-four-year-old accordion player, Peter Reno, who was hired by Vallone to entertain at his restaurant, the Sorrento. Reno testified Carlino told him to leave Houston, that he was the designated "fall guy" for the murder. Alleging that Carlino was a member of the dread Sicilian Mafia, Reno stated the grocer said, "The only way you can get out of that organization is in a bushel basket." Adding a touch of the macabre, Reno testified Carlino told him that as part of his initiation into the mob, he drank a glass of blood.

Reno told the jury that Carlino cautioned him, "I might as well tell you, if you don't leave town, I won't feel responsible for your life." Reno and his wife and four children fled Houston, returning briefly only to sell their house and furniture.

Then it was Percy's turn. Unlike the first trial, Carlino took the stand in his defense. Only after he was beaten and tortured for more than thirty-two hours did he make his confession, he told the jury. He added that Kern and Klevenhagen threatened to arrest his family and that he was afraid they also would be tortured.

The prosecution had earlier introduced in evidence three nude photographs of Carlino taken while he was in jail. The photographs showed no bruises on his body, but the grocer swore the photos had been taken before he was beaten. He denied any connection with Vallone's murder and said except for playing bingo at a church affair he had never gambled nor had he ever taken a drink of liquor in his life. If true, he was a unique World War II paratrooper.

He further testified he was a friend of Vallone's and had no reason to kill him, adding that he had never heard of the Mafia until he read about it in the newspapers after the murder.

The trial was recessed for a day after Percy allegedly slipped on the steps in the hotel lobby where he was staying

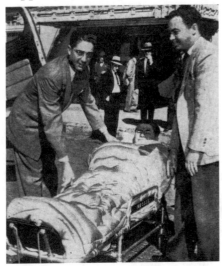

and injured his leg. A photograph in the *San Angelo Evening Standard* newspaper shows Percy lying on a stretcher, his head peeping out to face the camera from under what looks like an arctic comforter, which enveloped him from head to toe.

Doctors at a local hospital reported no broken bones, but the following day Percy entered the courtroom hobbling on crutches.

Percy, bundled like an Egyptian mummy, delayed the Carlino trial after he claimed he slipped on stairs and injured his leg.

97

Whether he was really injured or faking it is not difficult to determine. Percy's reputation for flamboyance and grandstanding caused skeptics to believe he wanted to strike a dramatic pose while pleading his client's case on crutches. Adding fuel to that theory were the events of a few days later when the attorney demonstrated great agility while dashing down the courthouse hallway.

When the trial recommenced, Carlino returned to the stand and presented the alibi that at the time of the murder he was visiting with his cousin, Jose Camara, a Spanish sailor whose ship was docked in the port of Houston. Foreman then presented in evidence a list of the crew of the Spanish freighter *Mar Negro*. On it was listed the name of an able bodied seaman named Jose Camarraera Camara. Foreman told the court the sailor could not confirm the alibi because his ship was somewhere at sea and they were unable to contact him.

After Percy rested the defense, to his utter surprise the state called a new witness. The district attorney's office had located the Spanish sailor named Jose Camarraera Camara. When this was announced, a newspaper reporter wrote, "Carlino blanched, the muscles in his jaw stiffened, but he said nothing. He quickly recovered his composure."

The pudgy, spectacled forty-nine-year-old sailor was located by the prosecution and brought in secret to the court after it was learned that his ship was docked at Brownsville, Texas. He was contacted through the efforts of the Spanish consul at that port.

Seemingly bewildered by all the hubbub, the sailor testified that he had never met Diego Carlino, had never heard of him, and as a Spaniard, he had no Italian cousins. Somewhat taken aback, Percy grilled the seaman, asking him if he had received money for his testimony. Vigorously denying this, the Spaniard plaintively asked Percy, "Tell me sir, how you get me in this?" Percy, shrugging, finally told the court, "This man is obviously not the same Jose Camara that Carlino had reference to."

During cross-examination and throughout the trial, Percy kept up a barrage of innuendos and accusations against Kern and Klevenhagen. At one point, Percy asked Kern why he handled Carlino so "roughly." Kern responded, "I was a lot nicer to him than you are being to me on this witness stand."

But Percy never let up. He told the jury that Kern was framing Carlino to win his election as sheriff. He charged that Kern and Klevenhagen forced Carlino to make a confession in order to get $5,000 in reward money for themselves. He accused both of them of torturing the defendant. He told the jury Klevenhagen was a liar. He accused state's witness Reno as being the real killer.

In summing up his case to the jury, Percy outdid himself in venom. He hobbled on his crutches up to the jury box and accused the two lawmen. "They tortured my client." Pointing his finger at each member of the jury, he shouted, "You too would confess if these pistol-packing, black-jack-wearing, handcuff-carrying, booted and spurred officers of the so-called law had decided you would be made to confess."

Dramatically pointing the finger of his outstretched arm at the two lawmen, Percy screamed, "I expose to you the KKK. Kern and Klevenhagen, they are the Ku Klux Klan of law enforcement. They are the Gestapo."

Both lawmen sat immobile. The blood drained from their faces. Their eyes stared like blue ice cubes. Spectators wondered, "How much abuse can these officers take?" They would soon find out.

After Foreman completed his four-hour vicious attack on Texas law officers and the prosecutor summed up his case, a confused jury retired to deliberate on a verdict. During the twelve-day trial, charges, countercharges, insults, and verbal smokescreens had so confused the actual facts that it was difficult to tell if it was Kern or Klevenhagen or Carlino who was on trial for the premeditated murder of Vincent Vallone.

At 6:25 on the evening of February 29, after less than one hour of deliberation, the jury found Carlino not guilty. After the verdict was read to a surprised and shocked courtroom, Mrs. Frances Carlino burst into tears and embraced her husband. Five young women in the courtroom applauded the verdict. Judge Sutton promptly fined them twenty-five dollars each. Law officers who crowded the courtroom were ashen-faced. Percy Foreman looked apprehensive. He asked the judge for "protection." As Percy left the courtroom he was escorted by a deputy sheriff instructed to protect him. As Percy hobbled on his crutches into the courthouse hallway, he saw Kern and Klevenhagen. Smirking, he made a sarcastic comment to the men. It was a mistake. It was finally too much.

The stoic demeanor the two lawmen maintained during days of insults cracked. Fists flying, they peppered Percy with blows to the face. The huge attorney, who may have weighed more than both of them combined, yelled, "Help me, help me." He threw away his crutches and started to run back into the courtroom when Johnny slapped him in the face, dumping him on his ponderous posterior.

As a crowd of 200 people gasped, Percy scrambled to his feet and ran into the courtroom while several deputies restrained the enraged Buster Kern and Johnny Klevenhagen. As Percy was escorted from the courtroom, he insisted that he be taken to the local hospital.

Kern and Klevenhagen appeared before the Corporation Court presided over by Judge Jimmie Keen and each pleaded guilty to simple assault. The judge fined them five dollars each. A large number of sheriff's deputies and local police officers asked if they could pay the fines, but the judge demurred. "I'm paying it myself," Judge Keen said as he handed two five-dollar bills to his court clerk.

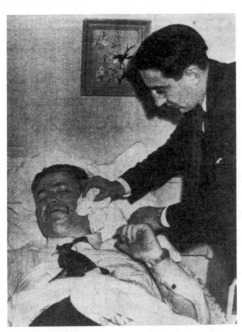

Diego Carlino, right, after being acquitted of murdering Vincent Vallone, tenderly cares for Percy Foreman after Johnny and Buster slapped him around.

Judge Sutton dismissed the incident, telling the press there was no contempt of his court since the incident took place in the courthouse corridor and not in his courtroom.

Percy spent the night at the local hospital. The following day the *San Angelo Standard*'s front page displayed a touching photograph showing Foreman, although fully clothed, lying on a hospital bed with an expression of excruciating pain. Diego Carlino, now acquitted of being a Mafia killer, was bending over him tenderly swabbing his fevered brow. The photo, however, showed no obvious damage to the Foreman jowls.

The following morning the *Houston Post* also had a front-page photograph showing Percy looking into a mirror with his face taped up like an Egyptian mummy. The caption read "Percy Foreman examines his wounds."

All in all it was a nasty affair. While no one can excuse police officers striking a defense attorney, one can understand it. Tough and stoic as they were, Kern and Klevenhagen were human. They were men who in the line of duty had been punched, shot at, who had spent sleepless nights, living on coffee and cigarettes while tracking down savage felons, who were away from their families for days while pursuing killers, rapists, burglars, and the assorted scum of the Texas underworld.

Then as a reward, for days they were publicly excoriated as liars, torturers, and crooks by Percy Foreman who, while influencing a jury, had no regard for truth or human decency. Although a few defense lawyers blathered about filing criminal charges against the two lawmen, Percy decided not to press charges.

While Johnny Klevenhagen maintained an icy silence about the affray, Buster Kern, because he had a political reputation to maintain, spoke out loudly. He told the Houston press corps:

"Nobody hit Foreman in the courtroom. There was nothing wrong with his leg. That was a sham. I've taken everything I can from him. He's insulted me and told vicious lies about me in front of the jury and the court. Every time we try a murder case, we have to be insulted and treated to his dirty tactics.

"Foreman admitted under cross-examination that he manufactured the name of an alibi witness (the Spanish sailor). There does not seem to be any law to protect a peace officer from Foreman's kind of vilification.

"I have no apologies to make. Foreman had a beating coming to him because of his tactics. Freeing Carlino was a bad verdict. But still we have let the Mafia know they can't operate in Harris County as long as I am sheriff."

Although undoubtedly biased, Buster's office reported that 100 telephone calls a day were pouring in celebrating the punch-out. Chief Deputy Sheriff E.B. Williams said, "Callers said they think Foreman has no respect for himself or anybody else and will resort to any tactics. They say he has no conception of truth and only assails the character of good people. A lot of people complained," the lawman said, "because Buster and Johnny didn't do a good enough job on Foreman."

At the conclusion of the trial, Carlino disappeared into the canyons of New York City. Nine months later he was indicted on a charge that he perjured himself during testimony. In March 1954 the indictment was dismissed by the Harris County district attorney on the grounds Carlino could not be found.

Although they lost the case, Buster and Johnny made good on their pledge that they would prevent the Mafia from gaining a foothold in Harris County. There are stories of not-so-gentle rebuffs to Mafioso arriving in Houston. One rumor had it that when dapper dresser Mickey Cohen, a former buddy of the once dreaded, now deceased gangster Bugsy Siegal, the founder of the mob-run Flamingo casino in Las Vegas, stepped off an airplane at Houston, he was met by the "Gold Dust Twins." He was escorted to a nearby hanger, his hat was pulled down over his eyes, the shoulder pads on his custom tailored suit were ripped, his garishly colored silk tie was tied into a knot, and his hair poking out from his busted hat was mussed. The two lawmen twigged his ears and told him Mafiosi were not welcome in Houston.

They put him on the next plane to Los Angeles with the admonition that the next time he came to Houston he would be returned in a pine box. Mickey never revisited

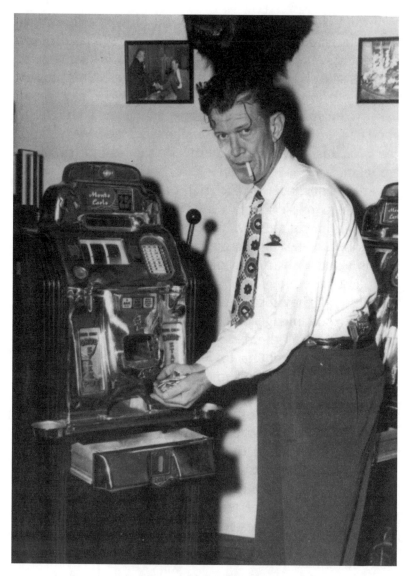

Harris County Sheriff Buster Kern checks out illegal slot machines
seized during raids on Houston bars.
(Photo courtesy of Houston Public Library)

Houston. He reputedly told a Los Angeles newspaper reporter, "Them Texas guys is nuts."

Through the years it became a tradition to meet touring members of the Cosa Nostra at the airport and extend the same greeting.

In later years, Johnny's son, John J. Jr., a premier lawman in his own right, was elected sheriff of Harris County, and the tradition was maintained. After almost half a century, the Mafia has never gotten a foothold in Harris County, and the Vallone killing was the only murder in Houston that was ever attributed to that underworld crime syndicate. It is a rather fine legacy from the "Gold Dust Twins."

CHAPTER 11

Such a Nice Young Man

Shortly before the Vallone murder, Johnny gave Buster a hand in playing nursemaid to the stars, the Hollywood version. The occasion was the grand opening of the Shamrock Hotel in Houston on St. Patrick's Day, March 17, 1949.

Glen McCarthy, the proud owner, turned the affair into an extravaganza that was a cross between a trip to Oz, the coronation of a Balkan king, and a mad scene from a Marx Brothers movie.

The wildcatter rented a fleet of airplanes and the Santa Fe Railroad's Super Chief to bring in more than a hundred Hollywood personalities including Pat O'Brien, Dorothy Lamour, Hugh Herbert, Van Johnson, Van Heflin, Edgar Bergen, Peggy Cummings, and radio star Ed Gardner. As one flickering star remarked when arriving at a Houston railroad station, "It was just a good clean drunk all the way."

There were also a scandal of starlets, a bevy of second bananas, and a glitter of assorted Euro-trash barons and earls who mingled with the governor of Texas and the nouveau riche of Texas oildom. For good luck, McCarthy had

2,500 shamrocks flown in from Ireland. The jewel of the day was the emerald, and they sparkled among earlobes, fingers, and necks. There were, of course, many diamonds. Johnny estimated the more than eleven hundred guests were sporting more than $10 million worth of baubles.

The gaudy display attracted a plentitude of jewel thieves, con artists, phony oil stock salesmen, and assorted hotel burglars. Johnny, along with the burglary and bunco squads of the Houston police, sheriff's deputies, and private security men, mingled with the elite in a successful effort to keep a raucous party from turning into mayhem. The bad guys were arrested on sight, hustled out of the hotel, and advised to get out of town or they would join a more permanent party cleaning the county jail.

The Shamrock party lasted for two weeks, and the hangovers must have been longer. After long nighttime vigils, Johnny was catching up on his sleep when he was called to Galveston to probe a bizarre murder.

There was a cool offshore breeze blowing at midnight, April 4, when Marvin Clark, owner of the C&M Food store, finished going over his accounts. He counted more than $400 in cash, then locked it in his small black steel box, tucked his .45-caliber pistol into a paper bag, stepped to the doorway, turned off the lights, and locked the door.

He sniffed the sea air as he carefully looked down the darkened streets. They were empty, but you could never be too sure. Recently there had been a series of store robberies in the area, and Clark was a cautious man. With the money box tucked under his arm he walked to his automobile, laid the bag with his pistol on the front seat next to him, got behind the wheel, and began the long drive home.

From time to time he glanced in the rearview mirror; there was no one following him. When he arrived at his Bay Shore Drive home about one o'clock in the morning, he breathed a sigh of relief. He parked the car in the drive, put the pistol in his pocket, and got out of the automobile. With one hand holding the moneybox, he held the car keys in his opposite hand and was about to lock the vehicle.

Suddenly, he saw a hooded figure leap out from the shrubbery beside the house. He let out a half yell, dropped his car keys, and reached for his pistol. He had it half out of the bag, but it was too late. The masked man fired a quick shot at point blank range, striking Clark in the heart. Clark stumbled, lurched forward, and with a dying grasp, ripped off the ski mask of his murderer. Then he fell dead.

Maddened at the resistance, the killer pumped four more bullets from a 7.65mm automatic into the prostrate body, emptying the magazine. Then he picked up Clark's .45-caliber pistol and, leaning over the body, fired two more bullets into Clark.

In a frenzy of sadism, the killer reversed the pistol and began to smash in the face of the dead grocer. He struck him so hard that pieces of the plastic handgrips broke off and scattered across the driveway. The killer rolled Clark's body over, picked up the moneybox, and fled into the night. He left the mask behind.

Awakened from a sound sleep by the sound of the gunfire, Mrs. Dora Clark stumbled from her bed and ran to the front door. Opening it, she saw the body of her thirty-two-year-old son in a spreading pool of blood, his face battered almost beyond recognition. Her screams and the gunfire awakened neighbors who telephoned the police.

When Galveston police officers arrived and searched the scene, they found only a khaki face mask, still clutched in the dead man's hand, two .32-caliber spent cartridge cases ejected from the killer's automatic pistol, pieces of a plastic handgrip, and smudged footprints in the flower bed by the side of the house. It was little to go on.

When Johnny arrived at the scene and reviewed the clues, he concluded the killer must have been known to Clark, hence the mask, and he must also have studied the merchant's movements. With these slim leads Klevenhagen began the tedious task of canvassing all the usual suspects—ex-cons who may have done the deed or who might know who did it and be ready to squeal in return for police favor. He canvassed long and hard but came up empty.

The viciousness of the attack at first convinced police that the murder must have been the result of a personal feud. But on investigation they found that Clark, an amiable man, had no enemies.

There were, however, two unsolved grocery store robberies that had occurred shortly before Clark's murder. Could there be a link? The Broadway Food Market was robbed of cash, several blank checks, and a .45-caliber revolver. And only a week previously the Hildebrand Grocery had been robbed, and in addition to cash an automatic pistol was stolen.

When Klevenhagen questioned the manager of the Hildebrand store, the man said, "The stolen weapon was a 7.65mm automatic pistol made in Czechoslovakia." There was, then, a possible link to the robberies, for Johnny, an expert on small arms, knew the Czech automatic was chambered for American .32-caliber automatic cartridges.

The manager volunteered he had bought the pistol from a friend in a nearby town who had used it for target practice. Klevenhagen bundled the agreeable manager into his automobile, and the two drove 100 miles to a country target range where the previous owner had fired the weapon.

At the range the two dropped to their hands and knees searching in the dirt for expended .32-caliber shell cases. They scrambled around for hours along the dusty firing line, picking up likely cases as if they were gold nuggets, for they knew if any of them matched those expended at the scene of Clark's murder, they could tie in both robberies with the murder weapon.

When they returned to Galveston with a bag of expended shell cases, Johnny sent them to the ballistic laboratories of the Texas Department of Public Safety in Austin to see if they compared with the markings on the casings found at the murder site.

The ranger got another break from a young fisherman. The lad walked into the Galveston police headquarters with a fishing spear, a freshly caught flounder, and a .45-caliber revolver. The boy said he was barefoot and spear fishing in nearby Offats Bayou, which is located near Clark's home.

"I just leaned over and speared the flounder laying on the bottom when I stubbed my toe on something hard, and I reached down and found this gun," he told police. It was soon identified as the weapon Clark had carried the night of the murder. It too, although badly rusted, was sent to the forensic lab in Austin.

A few days later the lab came up with a pair of solid clues. First, the cartridges found at the murder scene matched perfectly with some of those Johnny found at the firing range. This proved that the man who robbed Hildebrand's was the man who murdered Clark.

The second clue was the hood, which police described as greasy, olive drab in color, flannel lined, with large eyelets spaced around the crown. It looked something like a Roman centurion's helmet. More important, on the hood the science folk found strands of human hair. They added that the killer had had a recent scalp infection. As a result every ex-con in the area with a robbery or hold-up record was hauled into the Galveston police station, and a lock of his hair was clipped, catalogued, and sent to the Austin lab.

But none of them matched. Again the police were stymied. And although more than one hundred suspects had been questioned, the lawmen were no closer to finding the killer. For a while it seemed the Clark murder was a case that might never be solved.

Meanwhile, relatives of Clark made an extraordinary request; they asked Harris County Sheriff Buster Kern to help investigate the case. And so, the Gold Dust Twins were again working a tough case. Then they had another stroke of luck. One of the blank checks stolen from the Broadway store turned up at a local business, cashed by a young man named Jim Turner.

Police quickly traced Turner to a Texas City address, and Klevenhagen and Kern drove the short distance to the seaport city. The address was the home of Turner's parents, who told them their son had moved to a University of Houston trailer park in which students were housed. Their son, they said, was studying geology there and, they added, he would be glad to help them.

When they drove to the university, located the trailer, and met Turner, they found he was an amiable young man. Agreeing to accompany the two lawmen to Galveston, he told them he was working as an automobile mechanic at night while attending classes at the university during the day.

After they arrived at the Galveston police station and Turner was shown the check he had endorsed, he explained he had done some repair work on an automobile and the owner paid him with the check. "I never saw the man again," he said. Another dead end.

As Johnny arranged to have the young man driven back to Houston, one of the secretaries remarked, "He's such a nice young man. He couldn't be a killer." Perhaps.

Nevertheless, Johnny did a thorough investigation of Turner's background.

His full name was James Madison Turner III. He was twenty-six years old. When he was still a teenager he had married his high school sweetheart and they had a seven-year-old son. After the Pearl Harbor attack, Turner joined the Army Air Corps and volunteered as an aerial gunner. He was sent to England where he flew seventeen missions over those flack-filled skies. He was wounded three times and was awarded the Purple Heart with two clusters as well as an Air Medal for distinguished combat duty. In September 1945 he was discharged and returned to the waiting arms of his wife and child.

Returning to Texas City, he worked as an automobile mechanic until he enrolled at the University of Houston under the G.I. Bill and moved to the campus trailer park. To supplement the $120 a month received under the G.I. Bill, he worked as a automobile mechanic while his wife did sewing and ironing as well as selling cosmetics.

Neighbors said the couple were quiet, friendly, and hard working. Turner was, in all respects, a model of the returned veteran: a hero, a family man, straining to acquire a college education.

Again stalemated, weeks passed without a break in the case. There was one false lead after another, but they all broke down when the suspects' hair failed to match those strands found on the ski mask. Kern, frustrated, returned to his Harris County duties while Johnny doggedly followed one blind trail after another. Seven months went by and it seemed the case would never be solved.

Then on a morning late in November, Johnny got a telephone call from the chief of police in Texas City. A man whom we shall call Bill W. was arrested after shooting and wounding a man following an argument in a bar. "We took a

.45-caliber revolver from him. Maybe it will match one of the .45s involved in the Clark murder," the chief said.

Johnny rushed to Texas City and soon had the pistol identified as the one stolen from the Broadway Food Market. "Maybe I've got him at last," Johnny exulted. The Texas City police brought in Bill, a hard-nosed type, who refused to answer questions until Klevenhagen told him he was about to be charged with the murder of Marvin Clark and would soon find himself in Huntsville's death row.

At that Bill exploded, "What the hell are you talking about? I wounded a guy in a bar brawl. I never have heard of some guy named Marvin Clark."

When Johnny explained his pistol matched the one stolen from the Broadway Food Market and probably matched the slugs found in Clark, Bill broke out in a cold sweat. With shaking hands, he lit a cigarette, puffed deeply, and said, "Listen, I borrowed that gun from a friend of mine."

"Who?"

"He's a real nice guy named Jim Turner. He's a war hero and a family man. I don't know where he got the pistol, but he's a straight guy. He lives at the Houston University trailer camp for married vets."

Johnny decided it was time to again check out the person who was "such a nice young man." He drove to the university and knocked on the Turners' trailer door. There was no answer. On a hunch he drove back to Texas City to the home of Turner's parents. There he found Turner and his wife and child visiting over the Thanksgiving holidays.

Johnny told Turner, "I have a few questions about the man who gave you that check. Maybe you can help me clear it up. Would you mind coming down to the station with me?"

Turner, affable as usual, agreed. As he went out the door he waved to his mom, "I'll be back in time for some more turkey." He was mistaken.

When they reached the station, Klevenhagen took Turner into an interrogation room. He asked him again how he got the check stolen from the Broadway Food Market. Turner, seeming at ease, repeated his story about getting it in payment for an auto repair job.

The ranger then looked directly into Turner's eyes, "How did you get the .45 that was stolen from the Broadway store?"

Taken by surprise, Turner stammered, "I don't know what you are talking about."

"It's the same gun you loaned to Bill W."

Nervously, Turner stammered, "I don't know any Bill W."

"Well," Johnny replied, "he knows you." At that, in a loud voice, Johnny called out, "Come on in, Bill."

As Bill W. walked into the room, he looked at Turner and said, "Hi Jim."

Turner blanched and shouted, "I never saw this man before in my life."

"That's not what the folks at the Blue Ribbon Café will say. We put down a lot of brews there," Bill replied.

At that, Johnny waved Bill out of the room, looked into Turner's eyes with an intense stare, and slowly announced, "You are under arrest for the murder of Marvin Clark."

Terrified, Turner protested, "I don't know any Marvin Clark." Johnny produced a pair of scissors. "Then I'm glad you don't mind donating a few hairs to the cause of justice." Before Turner could object, he cut a few strands of his hair and carefully placed them in a small plastic vial.

"You made a big mistake," Johnny said, "when you left the ski mask behind after you killed Clark. We recovered hair from the mask. It's now in the lab at Austin. I'm sending your hairs there, and if they match, it will prove you are the killer. Why don't you save us a lot of trouble and tell the truth about what happened."

Turner began a long series of lies, but by now Johnny had learned from the owners of the Blue Ribbon Café that both Marvin Clark and Jim Turner had been frequent customers and had known one another. In fact, they said, the two men had been in the café and were talking together shortly before the murder.

After the stern ranger had spent several hours of questioning and punctured each alibi and denial of Turner's, the man finally slumped in his chair, holding his head in his hands. "I guess those hairs are going to match," he said, "I'll come clean."

Johnny then led him to the county attorney's office where Turner made a written confession of the murder of Marvin Clark. One of the clerks who typed up his statement of brutal, cold-blooded murder afterwards kept murmuring, "But he seemed to be such a nice young man."

The following morning Turner, in handcuffs, was placed in Johnny's automobile and gave him directions to where he dumped the 7.65mm automatic and the .45-caliber revolver that the young fisherman had found. The two, accompanied by Ranger Ed Oliver and followed by a flock of newspaper reporters and photographers, drove to Offats Bayou where, in the midst of flashbulbs and questions, he pointed to the spot where he had tried to dispose of all the incriminating evidence.

A huge crane with a powerful magnet was used to search the muddy waters of Offats Bayou. As darkness fell, the Galveston Fire Department brought searchlights to continue the effort throughout the night. But after almost three weeks of searching, they were never able to find the Czech pistol.

The lab in Austin, however, using powerful microscopes, enabled forensic experts to compare the hair found in the mask and the clippings from Turner's head. All agreed there was a perfect match.

Back at the county jail where Turner was being held, when he was told of the scientific match-up, he just shrugged. Finally, he said, "I need to go to the bathroom." Johnny nodded and pointed to the restroom and said, "Okay, go on." There was no window and only one door to the room so there was no way to escape.

Turner went into the restroom and shut the door. After a few minutes passed and Turner did not reappear, Johnny leaped up and, with an oath, ran to the door and flung it open. Slumped in a corner of the room was Turner, with a dazed look in his eyes, bleeding from both wrists. He had slashed them with a razor blade that he had concealed in a folded dollar bill. Quickly, Johnny wrapped both wrists tightly with towels and rushed Turner to nearby John Sealy Hospital where he was treated and sedated. Physicians said although he had lost blood, the wounds were not serious and he would recover quickly.

On Saturday, November 26, 1949, Turner was brought before a justice of the peace court where he pleaded guilty to the murder of Marvin Clark. By Sunday morning, fifteen hours later, however, when reporters visited him in his cell, he cried, "I didn't kill Clark." He claimed Texas Rangers John Klevenhagen and Ed Oliver and the chief of police of Texas City, "pushed me around and beat me up and I signed the confession under duress."

When one reporter asked why he slashed his wrists, Turner replied, "I did it to escape the pressure. I was tired of being pushed around. They made me sign the confession."

Klevenhagen responded that after Turner signed the confession and then cut his wrists, he was taken to the hospital, and doctors examined his entire body to make certain he had not been beaten.

Turner's most stalwart defender was his wife who "stood by her man." She told reporters, "I don't care what anyone says.... He couldn't do it.... The confession was beaten from him and he had no food, no water, and no sleep. He is a good man." It was a minority opinion.

Later Johnny told the newsmen that the matched hairs and the .45 pistol that linked both the Broadway Food Market and the Clark murder were all the evidence they needed to prove Turner guilty. "We don't really need a confession or the murder weapon," Johnny said, "Besides, denying confessions and faking suicide are routine criminal stuff."

After eight months of hard foot-slogging police work and the scientific competence of the Department of Public Safety's crime lab, the murderer of Marvin Clark was finally brought to justice. On December 16, 1949, Turner was indicted for murder with malice in Clark's death and charged with the robbery of the Broadway Food Market.

After being tried and convicted, Turner, in chains, was put on the bus to Huntsville State Prison to serve a thirty-year sentence. One of the detectives cynically remarked, "And he was such a nice young man."

CHAPTER 12

Of Jail Breaks and Barbers

One of a Texas Ranger's most difficult and sometimes most dangerous jobs is helping to apprehend escaped prisoners. With a large number of state prison farms located in his forty-six-county district, Klevenhagen had more than his share of that duty.

Chasing escaped prisoners often took him away from home for days at a time to the consternation of John Jr. So when the boy was nine years old, his dad gave him a broken pistol that wouldn't shoot and cautioned, "Now you must take care of your mom while I'm gone." The young fellow, feeling very grown up and responsible, slept with the weapon under his pillow, and the new responsibility seemed to ease the loneliness that came from missing his dad.

Psychology also played a part in dealing with convicts and often required an understanding and a creation of empathy between lawman and criminal that could work to the benefit of both. Sometimes, however, a more objective lesson was needed, and in later years John Jr. recounted how his dad handled one jail problem. During the 1950s, he said, at Ramsey Prison Farm in South Texas the inmates were grumbling about the food not being up to their epicurean tastes, or, most likely, they were bored and wanted to cause trouble.

During the day the prisoners were required to work in the fields either growing vegetables or chopping cotton. When they were rounded up in late afternoon for a return to their cells, a few took to hiding out in different areas of the farm. When they were missing from the afternoon countdown, the guards went into an uproar, sirens blasted, off duty guards came on the run, the Texas Rangers were summoned and sped to the scene, and everyone began to scour the farm area until the missing convicts were found, usually lounging in one of the fields.

In these cases the convicts weren't really trying to escape, they just wanted to discomfit their guards, foul up the prison routine, and in general drive the prison administration crazy. They thought it was a big joke. Johnny Klevenhagen, often aroused from a sound sleep or torn away from dinner with his family to jump into his auto and drive at a high rate of speed to the prison, was not amused.

One winter evening, summoned from a family dinner, he drove in the rain to Ramsey Prison Farm in a high state of annoyance. After he reached the prison, he joined the search and drove around the soaking prison fields for several hours until he spotted the missing convict. It had been warm and dry earlier in the evening when the convict launched his disappearing act, so in order to throw off the inevitable bloodhounds, he doffed his prison uniform and lay down naked in a cotton field.

When Johnny sighted him in his headlights, he was sitting in a pool of water, teeth chattering and body shivering. When he saw the ranger, he announced he was ready to return to his dry and warm prison cell, but Johnny, a little curtly, said, "You got your ass out here, you can damn well get it back where it belongs," and started to drive away. When the prisoner begged for a lift, Johnny relented but made him ride on the front fender of the automobile while he drove back to the cellblock.

Arriving there, he told the guard to turn on all the lights in the prison yard. Then he drove into the yard, telling the prisoner to remain bare-butted on the fender. While all the hard-core inmates looked on, Johnny drove the miscreant around and around the prison yard in the cold and the freezing drizzle until he "nearly froze his ass off." Then he let him return to the haven of his dry and warm cell.

On another occasion a convict slipped away from guards while working on the prison farm. After an all-night search, bloodhounds traced him to a large tree in the area. When Johnny and the guards arrived, they saw the man perched six feet up on a thick limb. After they had restrained the yapping and frothing hounds, Johnny looked up and shouted to the convict, "Get your ass down from there." Stubbornly the man repeatedly refused to come down and remained perched on the limb.

Texas Rangers are nothing if not innovative in their work. Johnny smiled, picked up his .30-caliber rifle, drew a careful bead, and rapidly fired half a dozen shots into the base of the convict's tree limb, which collapsed from the impact of the bullets. The convict came tumbling down, landing on his rump, after which he was returned to his cell, where, for a few days, he found it more comfortable to sleep on his stomach.

According to a rather incompetent burglar named James Lyles, who at that time was imprisoned at the Ramsey Unit, "That ended the nonsense the hard noses were causing in the prison." Lyles, who John Jr. said was a "good barber but a lousy burglar" was an example of the symbiosis that often occurs between police officers and out-laws. Lyles had been sent to jail by John Sr. on a burglary charge and then was later sent to the penitentiary for another bungled burglary by John Jr. when he was a Harris County deputy sheriff.

In later years after John Jr. had been elected sheriff of Harris County and John III had grown to manhood, the by now old barber, still in jail, made a request of the sheriff. "Bring Ranger John's grandson by. I'd like to be able to say that I've cut the hair of three generations of Klevenhagens." It was a request to be honored, so the sheriff took his son, now a practicing attorney in Houston, to the prison barber-shop, where Lyles duly gave him a very good haircut. "Sometimes," John Jr. said, "you do a favor for an old con."

In that vein, Johnny Sr.'s wife, Viola, remarked, "Every year we received dozens of Christmas cards from criminals Johnny had arrested. Many of them came from the state prison farms. Johnny said it was because he treated them fairly. And many of them were people who had never before been treated fairly by anyone." To a person unfamiliar with lawmen, it might seem strange that a man with a reputation for unflinching toughness and courage could also have a reputation among criminals as a man who never broke his word and never betrayed a confidence. But that is the stuff of which Texas Rangers are made.

On rare occasions when he had a respite from man hunting, Johnny took his son deer hunting. John Jr. recalls back in 1949 when he was nine years old, he shot his first deer. "When we got back to camp Dad said, 'Your work isn't finished, now you have to gut it and clean it out because this deer is for eating and it's a family rule, you never shoot anything you can't eat.'"

Viola said when Johnny Jr. was ten years old, late one evening Johnny received a call informing him there had been an escape at Angleton State Prison. Junior begged to go along with his dad and surprisingly got his wish.

When they got to the prison, Johnny said, "Stay in the car," and joined other officers in the search. Junior was eager to help and created a minor sensation when he saw a man in prison garb and yelled, "There's one of them escaping." As lawmen rushed to the scene they found the escapee was a trustee helping in the search. It was one of the very few mistakes John Jr. ever made as a crime buster. Viola, however, commented, "It was the beginning of a time when I had to worry about the safety of both of them."

Some prison escapes became life and death matters. Jedidiah Brown was sentenced to die in "Old Sparky," a convict term for the state's electric chair, for two cold-blooded murders. Unfortunately, his sentence had been commuted to life imprisonment. He was hoeing cotton in the sultry heat at Ramsey State Prison Farm late one afternoon when a mounted guard rode up too close to him. With a savage lunge, Jedidiah swung his hoe, striking the guard in the head and knocking him out of the saddle.

As the guard fell prostrate, Jedidiah grabbed the horse's reins, swung into the saddle, dug his heels into the mount's flank, and galloped westward towards the Brazos River. The Brazos, usually a mildly flowing stream, speeds up, deepens, and spreads out near its mouth on the Texas Gulf Coast. The current flows swiftly over treacherous mud flats and sandy sinkholes that can suck down an unwary horse and rider.

Reaching the river, Jedidiah started to ease his horse near the water, but the beast shied, let out a frightened whinny, and fought the bit as the convict jerked on the reins. Giving up on the spooked horse, he dismounted with a curse, walked to the riverbank, and for a moment stared at the 200-yard-wide quick-flowing stream of muddy water.

Then with a shrug, he plunged into the river and, exerting all the swimming power he could muster, fought his way across to the west bank.

Meanwhile, back at the prison farm, a posse was quickly formed and a dozen angry men on horseback began a pursuit of the fleeing murderer. They also telephoned Johnny Klevenhagen at his Houston office, and the ranger jumped into his automobile and drove at breakneck speed fifty miles to the west bank of the Brazos. This was a bad one, Johnny thought. Brown was considered to be a psychotic killer, and he had to be caught quickly before someone paid for his escape with his life.

Earlier the posse had tracked Jedidiah to the river's east bank and observed his footprints in the soft sand leading to the river. Prison Guard Captain Joe McGill, an excellent horseman, plunged his steed into the swirling waters and, after being whirled downstream a few hundred yards, finally managed to reach the west bank.

As Johnny arrived at the west side of the river, he began driving along the bank until he spotted McGill. On foot, the two searched along the slippery riverbank until they saw a lone farmhouse. Together, guns drawn, the two lawmen slipped up on the dwelling perched at the edge of a thick strand of timber. They were too late.

A hysterical farmer's wife ran out to meet them. Between frightened sobs she told them Jedidiah had smashed open her farmhouse door while her husband was away. As she rushed to the front of the house at the sound of the breaking door, she came face to face with the desperate convict. "He knocked me down," she cried, "then he ransacked the house until she found my husband's .30-30 Winchester carbine, then he took the gun and ran out of the house." She pointed to a small stream flowing nearby, "He ran upstream," she said.

While McGill used the woman's telephone to alert the posse to their position, Johnny, rifle in hand, headed toward the stream on the run. After he had dashed more than a hundred yards up the stream, he caught a glimpse of Jedidiah. When he came closer, the convict stepped from behind a tree, and as Johnny shouted, "Don't do it," Jedidiah fired a shot that whipped by the ranger's head. As he levered the Winchester to fire again, Klevenhagen fired his rifle. The bullet struck Jedidiah in the head, hurling him backward into the stream. He was quite dead and Johnny, again, giving a criminal the first shot, was again lucky to be alive.

McGill heard the shots and came panting up the stream. "Here's your escaped convict, Captain," Johnny said. With Klevenhagen lifting Jedidiah's arms and McGill his legs, the two lawmen hauled the body back to the ranger's automobile. Loading him into the back seat, they started to drive back to Ramsey when Johnny noticed he was low on gasoline. They pulled into a service station, but as the attendant started to fill the tank, he noticed the man propped up in the back seat with a bloody hole in the middle of his forehead.

As the startled attendant leaped backward, Johnny said, "Don't worry he won't hurt you. He won't hurt anyone ever again."

CHAPTER 13

The Chicago Chums

Two high school chums from Chicago, Arthur Henry Jung and Raymond Shaw, were bumming around the country doing odd jobs. Then in the spring of 1950 they arrived in the South Texas town of Jourdanton. There they got jobs working on a pipeline construction project designed to transport propane and butane products from refineries in the area.

The pay was good, the people were friendly, but the work was hard and the boiling hot Texas summer was coming on. Early in April, sweat soaked and tired, the two husky twenty-one-year-old Midwesterners concluded there must be easier ways to make some money. Pondering over too many beers in a rundown honky-tonk, they decided robbery was a much more desirable way to riches than breaking their backs on pipeline construction.

They needed to make a big score so they could return to Chicago with greenbacks bulging in their pockets. But who to rob? Who in little Jourdanton would have lots of money? More important, who would be easy or helpless? After pondering these weighty questions over more beers and fuzzier minds, they decided on the man they called the "Old Cowboy."

His name was Waddell L. Rhodes, a sixty-one-year-old pipeline welder, whose country ways and cowboy dress led to his nickname. Jung later said, "Everybody knew he had a lot of money because he lived on thirty cents a day and saved his salary." The two masterminds (both were high school graduates and Jung had a semester in Purdue University) set up a surveillance just like it was done in the gangster movies. On payday they followed the old fellow to the Jourdanton State Bank where they observed him depositing his paycheck.

Since the pipeline job had been going on for the better part of a year, they reasoned he must have a bundle in his account. But they must make sure; Jimmy Cagney, Humphrey Bogart, and George Raft always got the straight dope before pulling a job. So one day, on some excuse, they left the job early and went to the Jourdanton State Bank. It would be very simple. They would just ask the bank people how much money Rhodes had in his account.

Entering the bank lobby, they spied a pretty, young brunette teller, and oozing charm (they were both good-looking young men), they engaged her in conversation. "Say," Jung said, "An old buddy of ours, Waddell Rhodes, banks here. I bet he's got a bundle with your bank. Can you tell us how much he's got in his account?"

The young lady smiled; they seemed like real nice fellas, she thought, but they were awfully naive. However, with South Texas courtesy, she merely grinned and said, "That information is confidential. I can't tell you how much he has." Jung shrugged, waved a cheery good-bye, and the two left the bank. They were not annoyed they had not gotten their answer to that most important question. Shaw opined,

"The Old Cowboy must really have a lot of money in there if it's *confidential*."

The next day at lunch break, they sidled up to Rhodes, who was eating his thirty-cent sandwich, and struck up a conversation.

A friendly man, Rhodes told them that his hometown was the little hamlet of Hockley, which was almost a suburb of Houston. He had given over his house to his sister and her family, and he lived in a small trailer parked on the property. "She needs the room and I'm a bachelor, and I'm perfectly comfortable in the trailer and I enjoy the privacy," he said.

Before they went back to work, Rhodes gave the boys his address. "When the job is over, if you fellas are near Houston, come by and pay me a visit." The two assured him they would indeed pay him a visit.

Within a few days the construction project was completed and Rhodes waved good-bye to Jung and Shaw as he drove off to Hockley. The two returned to their favorite honky-tonk for a planning session. They reasoned he would have all his money in cash, but since this was a Friday he could not get to the bank in Hockley until Monday. "We have to move quickly while he's still got his money in cash," Jung said. "We'll hit his trailer Sunday night," Shaw stated.

Just in case the old man caught them in the act and started to fight back, Jung sawed a two-foot piece off a heavy wooden shovel handle. It would, they believed, make a good club. With their plans complete, the pair drove northeast 200 miles to Hockley.

On the dark, humid night of April 16, the two reached the little town and pulled their auto up near the Rhodes' residence. Then they quietly crept up on the darkened trailer. Either Rhodes was away or he was asleep. If he was gone, they would leisurely search the trailer for his bonanza; if he was home, well then, they would use their wooden blackjack.

Crouched by the trailer, Shaw turned the handle on the door; it squeaked a little but opened, and the two slipped inside. As they entered, one of them bumped a pot that went clattering to the floor. Rhodes, lying in bed, let out a grunt, opened sleep-blurred eyes, and groped about until he switched on the bedside light. As the light went on, Jung leaped to his bedside and smashed him in the head with his club.

The spade handle, however, proved ineffective as a blackjack, and Jung had to strike the aged welder more than a dozen times as the man thrashed about still half asleep trying to dodge the furious blows. Finally, Shaw grabbed his arms and held them behind his back as Jung hammered away at Rhodes' bloody head. Beaten to a pulp, Rhodes finally sank to the floor, unconscious.

Using only the dim light of the bedside lamp, the two searched the trailer from stem to stern. All they found, however, was $45 in cash in the man's wallet. Cursing their luck and realizing they had clubbed a man to death for a pittance, the blood-splattered pair slunk out of the trailer and back to their auto. Early Sunday morning they drove north to Chicago. At least, they thought, there was no way that they could be caught.

Sometime after the two chums left the trailer, Rhodes regained some measure of consciousness. More by instinct than reasoned thought, he crawled from the trailer, fell to the ground, and on all fours tried to propel himself to his house to rouse his sister. The blood-soaked trail marking his desperate efforts ended some ten yards from the house where exhausted he sprawled on the lawn, gasped, and died.

Much later that morning, Rhodes' ten-year-old grand-niece, dressed in her churchgoing Sunday best, stepped out of her home, looked out over the lawn, and screamed. She ran back into the house, crying, "It's Uncle Waddell, he's all bloody and hurt bad." As other family members rushed out, they saw Waddell dressed only in his underwear, lying in a pool of blood. After quieting the hysterical little girl, they phoned for an ambulance and the police.

At the Klevenhagen home the family was gathered around the breakfast table talking about how they would spend the rare day when Johnny was not out on a case. Then the telephone rang. Sheriff Buster Kern was on the line with the news of another brutal murder, and quickly the ranger was en route to Hockley. Arriving there, Klevenhagen organized a search party to beat the bushes in the surrounding area to search for a murder weapon, then he put in a call for the state prison bloodhounds. The search proved helpful; the bloodhounds didn't.

By late morning, deputies found the red-stained shovel handle lying in a ditch near a railroad track. Klevenhagen brought it into the trailer and identified it as the murder weapon when a sliver of wood on the bed matched a ripped off place on the handle. Also, there was a smudge of silver paint that had rubbed off on a shelf over the bed. The smudge matched the color of the silver paint job on the club. Much later laboratory tests showed the blood on the weapon matched Rhodes's.

In the early afternoon the bloodhounds got into the act. They sniffed around the trailer for several minutes and then with enthusiastic yelping started straining at their leashes. Down the street the dogs ran, winding their handlers, until after they had dashed several blocks they pulled up and began whining and pawing at the door of a local beer joint.

To the startled dismay of the Sunday afternoon boozers, hounds followed by a dozen police officers with drawn guns burst into the little barroom. Some of the customers were half groggy from too many longnecks, and others were half scared out of their wits by the pack of snarling hounds rubbing sniffing noses against their legs while slobbering and snorting loudly.

The twenty beer drinkers in the bar were questioned extensively by Klevenhagen and sheriff's deputies, and some of the more raunchy ones were given lie detector tests. Klevenhagen dismissed the group as innocent, at least as far as the crime against Rhodes was concerned. After many inquiries in Hockley, the ranger determined the man had no local enemies and indeed was well liked by everyone. The only explanation for the behavior of the dogs was that Rhodes had often been a customer of the local beer joint, and the hounds must have picked up his scent from the trailer to the bar.

After several more days of investigation in Hockley turned up neither clue, nor motive, nor suspect, Johnny took up the trail in Jourdanton. With a population of not much more than a thousand, it was inevitable that Klevenhagen would check out the local bank. When he encountered the bright young teller at State Bank, she recounted how two men had inquired about Rhodes' finances. "They were young, good-looking, and gave the appearance of men who worked in construction," the young lady told the ranger, and she said she was sure they didn't live in Jourdanton. She said she would be able to identify them from a photograph.

After further inquiries, Johnny located a local pipeline worker who had taken a number of snapshots of his buddies on their fifty-man construction crew. Klevenhagen took the snapshots to the bank teller, who immediately picked out the two personable young men so interested in their friend's bank account. After a trip to the construction company's office, Johnny found a foreman who was able to put names to the men in the photos and give him their home addresses. A day later Johnny was on an airplane to Chicago.

In the Windy City he cut a picturesque figure at police headquarters with his boots, Stetson, Ranger badge, and Texas drawl. The Chicago cops knew Texas Rangers from reputation, and Johnny looked the archetype of the force. They were most cooperative, and in a short time they located Raymond Shaw working as a painter's helper in a downtown building. On June 11, 1950, accompanied by a Chicago policeman, Klevenhagen went to the building and found Shaw standing on a ladder painting a wall. He shouted, "Are you Raymond Shaw?" The painter looked down and his heart sank as he saw a tall, flinty-eyed man in boots and ten-gallon hat, with a .45 stuck in his belt. At that moment he knew it was all over. "I realized," Shaw said later, "Texas had caught up with me."

As Johnny was hauling Shaw to the Chicago police station, Sheriff Buster Kern was arresting Arthur Jung in Indianapolis where he had gone to live with his mother. He was pumping gasoline in a filling station when Kern and a bevy of local police officers took him into custody.

Two days later Shaw and Jung, each blaming the other for the crime, were signing confessions in the Houston sheriff's office. It had taken Johnny less than two months of plugging away at routine police work plus several thousand miles of travel to break the case. It helped that Shaw and Jung were as stupid as they were vicious.

Almost a year later on May 23, 1951, the two pled guilty to murder in a Houston district court. Jung's mother and aunt journeyed from Indianapolis to be at his side and during the routine proceedings flooded the court with tears begging for mercy for the two boys. A mother's tears are hard to refuse by old-time Texans, and the judge declined to sentence them to be executed but instead sentenced them to life in prison.

As the verdict was announced, the two women again burst into tears. Jung's mother, thanking the judge, said, "We prayed so hard and we are so happy that you were merciful." Jung and Shaw, perhaps in their ignorance of life in Texas prisons, were also relieved. Shaw told reporters, "I'm glad it's over. I haven't been able to get a good night's sleep since we killed the old cowboy."

Klevenhagen answered laconically, "You'll have plenty of years to sleep from now on."

CHAPTER 14

Three Punks and a Gorgeous Carhop

The first two robberies went down easy. They got $120 when they stuck up Murphy's Pharmacy and $70 from the gasoline station. Then they picked up Wanda, piled into the old 1942 Dodge, and drove from Houston to San Antonio. They planned to live it up there and have fun before they hit the place "Pegleg" Johnson had picked out for the big heist. Then, with plenty of money, they would drive to the coast for a long, wild party.

When they arrived in San Antonio at three o'clock Thursday morning, March 8, 1951, they were all pooped out after the two stick-ups and the 200-mile drive. So Richard Thorbus, Bobby Miers, Leroy "Pegleg" Johnson, and a gorgeous carhop, whom we will call Wanda (because that's not her real name) pulled into a motel, crowded into one room, and slept until noon.

Then they got up and drove downtown where they went on a shopping spree, buying fancy nylon cowboy shirts, brightly colored ties, and fancy, expensive socks. They drove out to the zoo and, laughing and joking, wandered past the monkey island, the steel-barred cages housing the big cats, and the pool containing sleepy-eyed alligators. Pegleg, the leader and planner of the group, decreed, "Let's go horseback riding," so they drove to the stables at Brackenridge Park.

Later the stable owner was able to identify all four of them. He particularly remembered Pegleg because "He had an artificial limb, so I rented him a very gentle horse." After a long ride around the park, by late afternoon the quartet had worked up a huge appetite. They drove downtown, parked, and entered Lee's Café on South Presa Street. There, according to the manager, they gorged themselves on chicken fried steaks, Mexican dinners, hamburgers, French fries, and milk.

They joked about how they had met. Miers and Pegleg had become acquainted when they, as teenagers, were both incarcerated in the same federal reform school in Washington, D.C. A few years later they met up again in the Houston city jail where Miers was booked on a burglary investigation and Pegleg was in the same bullpen sobering up after being arrested for public drunkenness. Thorbus, also arrested for being drunk in public, was chucked in with them.

The following day all were released and Miers, who knew Wanda, used his remaining funds to bail her out of jail where she was being held for stabbing an all-too-attentive boyfriend. Joining together, the four then hijacked the Houston pharmacy and the gas station and began their trip to San Antonio.

It was twilight when the well-stuffed young people left the café and drove to the business site that Pegleg had picked out for their big stick-up job. But for some unknown reason they decided not to strike there. They agreed there were better pickins in Corpus Christi so they drove to the highway leading to that port city.

One of the men, probably Pegleg, started passing out "goofballs," a phenobarbital derivative, and soon all four were sky high. They were driving south when they came upon a sign pointing to the Hilltop Garage and Filling Station. It was a big, rambling, prosperous-looking place, and Pegleg said, "Let's hijack the Hilltop." The other two men immediately agreed, but Wanda warned, "You better not do it. Them country people will fight for their money. Don't do it."

Pegleg, who was driving, said, "Oh shut up, Wanda." As he pulled in front of the Hilltop, he told the other two men, "You guys stick 'em up. I'll keep the engine running. Wanda, stay in the car."

Thorbus, packing a cheap 7.65mm Belgian automatic pistol, and Miers, carrying a .38-caliber revolver, got out of the car and walked into the Hilltop establishment. The place was more than a garage and filling station and included a liquor store and a farm supply store with living quarters in the rear. Looking over the place, Thorbus and Miers figured there would be a juicy haul.

As they entered the store, the owner, fifty-seven-year-old Edmund Niemann, smiled and said, "Good evening boys, what can I do for you?" Both men flourished their weapons and replied, "Give us your money." Niemann, surprised, went to the cash register and opened it. Thorbus reached in and pulled out six dollars and a personal check, the entire contents of the register.

"Where's the rest of it?" Miers yelled. When Niemann said that was all the money he had, Miers started cursing and beating him on the head with his pistol. Thorbus said, "I'll get the bastard's wife. Then he'll give it up," and rushed to the living quarters in the back of the store. He found Mrs.

Niemann calmly sitting at her dining room table eating supper. Shoving the gun in her face, he said, "Come with me, I want the money," and forced the frightened women to walk to the store's business office.

At the same time, Andrew Sendemer, a thirty-eight-year-old county employee, his wife, and their five-year-old son were in their pickup driving toward San Antonio to go bowling. As they approached the Hilltop complex, Andrew turned to his wife and said, "Let's stop here, I want to get some gas."

After he turned off the road and pulled up to the gasoline pumps, he was met by Miers, who pointed a pistol at the head of Mrs. Sendemer, saying, "This is a holdup; get out of the truck." Miers marched the little family into the store office where Mrs. Niemann was screaming as Thorbus was beating her husband about the head, cursing and yelling, "Where's your money?"

The sight of the elderly man being beaten was too much for Andrew to bear, and he charged Miers and tried to grab the pistol out of his hand. Miers shot him through the heart. But as Andrew fell, he clutched Miers' coat, ripping it off.

At the shot, battered as he was, Niemann attempted to come to Andrew's aid and charged Miers. Thorbus shot him in the leg and smashed his head with his pistol butt.

As the two horrified wives screamed and the little boy burst into sobs, Miers, hearing Thorbus' shot, panicked. Somehow, he got the impression that it was Thorbus who was shot. He ran out of the building screaming, "They shot Thorbus. Let's get out of here." As Miers jumped into the Dodge, Pegleg drove off fast. They had gone half a block when Wanda, looking out of the rear window, saw Thorbus back at the Hilltop, frantically waving.

She alerted Pegleg who made a 180-degree turn, nearly overturning the Dodge, and raced back to pick up an agitated Thorbus. They headed for Houston at high speed using back roads. As they were approaching the small farming village of Elmendorf, Pegleg, who was rattled and driving too fast, lost control and ran the Dodge into a ditch, where it stuck fast.

After Pegleg fruitlessly tried to drive the car back on the road, the quartet stood around the auto in a high state of panic. Miers kept muttering, "I think I killed that guy," while Pegleg lamented, "We only got six dollars."

Suddenly Pegleg announced, "We need to take the Thieves Oath to each other. If anyone of us gets caught, we swear not to tell on the others. We'll all kill anyone who violates the oath." Solemnly, while standing in the darkened ditch, the four raised their right hands and swore to be true to one another.

Shortly afterwards an automobile driven by Mrs. Helen Flores, an Elmendorf farmer's wife, came upon the scene. She saw four people standing by an old Dodge, which was cocked at a strange angle in a ditch by the shoulder of the road. Mrs. Flores stopped, and after Pegleg asked for help, she pulled up behind the Dodge and, shifting into second gear, managed to push the Dodge back up onto the roadway. Thanking her instead of killing her, they drove off into the night.

They planned to return to the Houston area on a great circle route by swinging south on back roads to Victoria and then northeast to the San Jacinto Battleground State Park. After driving all night they arrived there Friday morning and spent most of the day touring the site of Sam Houston's victory over the Mexican army in 1836, almost 115 years before to the day.

They crowded into the tourist elevator and rode to the top of the San Jacinto Monument. Then they made a tour of the old battleship *Texas* moored near the battleground. It had been quite a holiday.

Soon, according to Wanda, the three men started to argue, each blaming the others for the botched robbery and murder. The only thing they agreed on, she said, was that they pledged they would never be taken alive.

While the three men were hopped up on goofballs, Wanda, realizing the mess she had gotten herself into, became frightened. When the group drove to Houston late that afternoon, they split up. Thorbus and Miers said they were going to pose as fishermen and hide out near Seabrook, a small boating and fishing village on Galveston Bay. Pegleg said he would hole up in his room in Houston.

Wanda returned to her Houston apartment and, clutching her five-year-old daughter, cried for a long time. She knew she faced a murder charge, which would result with either a date with "Old Sparky" or a long prison sentence. "I'll never see my daughter again," she moaned. Then she remembered that while she was in jail she had heard from other inmates that a Texas Ranger named Klevenhagen was a man who could be trusted to be fair and understanding.

Perhaps he can help me, she thought; if not, she believed she was doomed. Her hopped-up and stupid companions, she knew, would soon be caught by police, and, stupid Thieves Oath notwithstanding, she would be implicated. She picked up the telephone and dialed the number of the Harris County Courthouse. "Could I please speak to Texas Ranger Klevenhagen?" she asked.

Klevenhagen had been on the case since early Friday evening, working the one solid clue left behind at the murder scene. Andrew Sendemer had not died in vain. With Miers' bullet in his heart, he held a death grip on the coat of his assailant and ripped it off as he fell. The coat somehow ended up under his body, and Miers in his panic ran off without retrieving it.

Inside the coat was a Houston clothing store label. When the San Antonio police informed Klevenhagen of the clue, that night he traced the sale of the coat from the store manager to the clerk who, by a stroke of great luck, remembered the name of the man who purchased it. Within minutes, Klevenhagen and Buster Kern arrived at the Houston home of a startled man named Miers, and guns drawn they put him under arrest.

They soon found, however, that the man had no police record and had an ironclad alibi. So they believed him when he told them, "I loaned my coat to my brother, Bobby Miers." Within only a few hours of the murder, Klevenhagen had the name of one of the bandits. His whereabouts and the names of his accomplices, however, remained unknown.

When Johnny returned to his office, he saw a note by his telephone saying, "Wanda called," and a return number. Calling her, he quickly arranged a meeting at which time the pretty carhop relayed the entire story of the robbery. Johnny put out a bulletin giving names, descriptions, and probable locations of the three Hilltop killers. Before midnight, police in the Seabrook area started hunting for Thorbus and Miers, and Houston police scoured sleazy boardinghouses and beer joints for Pegleg Johnson.

Miers and Thorbus were vicious, but they were not smart; in fact, they were exceedingly stupid. They rented a motel room in Kemah, a small town near Seabrook, and bought two bamboo fishing poles. In their doped-up state, they purchased a Texas and a British flag and draped them over the side windows of their automobile so, they later said, "No one could look in and see us." Then they tied the fishing poles onto the roof of the Dodge. This, they thought, disguised them as honest fishermen. So much for "speed" as a drug which sharpens mental perceptions.

State Highway Patrolmen H.W. Smith and W.R. Thompson were patrolling along the Seabrook Road when they saw a strange apparition coming down the road. An automobile was being driven down a busy highway with the driver's vision obscured because both front side windows were covered with flags. It was bizarre, even for weekend fishermen who had indulged in too much lager. Smith and Thompson flashed their lights, curbed the Dodge, and approached the car, service revolvers at the ready. The two men inside matched the description of the Hilltop killers, and a quick search of their automobile located a Belgian automatic pistol in the glove compartment. Swiftly the two men, who had remained docile, were handcuffed and driven to the Houston sheriff's office where they were introduced to Johnny Klevenhagen.

Johnny interrogated the two individually, told them of the overwhelming evidence against them, and convinced them it was in their best interest to tell the truth. Johnny was a very convincing interrogator, and soon he had written confessions from both men. "Thieves Oath," notwithstanding, each of the two blamed the others for the crime.

Tipped off by Wanda as to Pegleg's address, at six o'clock Saturday morning, Klevenhagen arrested a sleepy-eyed Pegleg who, unlike the others, denied any involvement in the Hilltop robbery.

After Wanda came into Johnny's office Saturday morning and gave a long written statement about the crime and agreed to be a state's witness, the ranger promised her she would be treated generously by the court in exchange for her cooperation.

Sunday morning the three men were handcuffed, chained together, and transported by police van to San

Antonio where they were booked for murder and placed in the Bexar County jail. Johnny drove Wanda to San Antonio where she remained in custody in the women's ward of the jail.

There, the green-eyed, auburn-haired, glamorous-looking, nineteen-year-old carhop, already a divorced mother with a five-year-old daughter, retold her story and posed for photographs for enthralled newsmen.

The Hilltop Gang, as they were called, was quite a foursome. Richard Dean Thorbus, twenty, had been in trouble with the police all his young life. As a pre-teenager he was sent to a juvenile reformatory for stealing an automobile, and while there, he badly beat up a guard in a failed escape attempt. A few years later he was successful in breaking out and stole a jeep from an army recruiting station. He was finally arrested in California and served time in prison there. Released, he came to Houston where he was suspected of involvement in a number of robberies.

Tall, stooped, and slack-mouthed, wearing a gaudily colored sport shirt, Thorbus remained defiant to newspaper reporters, telling them, "Somebody ought to tell those Dutchmen not to jump guys with guns. They ought to wise up." He shrugged, "It's hopeless now. I'll get the electric chair." Sadly, he was mistaken.

Leroy "Pegleg" Johnson, twenty-four, burly, foul-mouthed, also with a long police record, defiantly told reporters, "I didn't have nothin' to do with it." Nervously combing and re-combing his slicked-down black hair and chewing gum, he said a train ran over his leg when he was four years old. After Thorbus identified him as the driver of the getaway car, he snarled, "I'm sorry I ever saw that punk."

Robert E. Miers, nineteen, was wearing a chartreuse sports shirt, looking frightened, and chewing gum like a starving man eating a roasted chicken. He described how Andrew Sendemer charged him, they struggled, he said, and "the gun just went off. I'm sorry, I guess," he stated reluctantly.

On Monday Mr. and Mrs. Niemann, Sendemer's widow, and Mrs. Flores identified the quartet. When Sendemer's son was asked if he could identify the man who murdered his father, the little boy burst into tears.

The four were formally charged with murder and led to cells. Jailers removed a cursing Johnson's artificial leg, saying, "We have to do it. This could make quite a weapon. You could beat a man to death with it." In perhaps a more practical vein, the jailers found a razor blade concealed in the leg.

As the cell door slammed on Thorbus, he growled, "If Sendemer would have minded me and lay on the floor, he wouldn't be in the grave. Those people that jump up like Superman just don't know nothin'. He should have minded his own business." So much for contrition.

In subsequent trials, Pegleg Johnson, who finally confessed, drew a thirty-year jail sentence; Thorbus got life in prison. Johnny, true to his word, got Wanda off with a five-year sentence and soon, out on parole, she was reunited with her daughter. Robert Miers, the man who shot Sendemer to death, was sentenced to die in the electric chair.

Bill Hauck, later to become sheriff of Bexar County and who back in the 1930s rode in the sidecar when Johnny was a motorcycle officer in the San Antonio Police Department, gave Klevenhagen credit for the quick arrest of the Hilltop Gang. "It was his quick work that identified and helped locate the gang, enabling officers to make the quick arrests. Johnny was always fast on sharing information with others, and it paid off in this case."

But the Hilltop saga wasn't over. In late 1952, while in the death house, Bobby Miers found God; or at least he said he did. It started when a jail chaplain "led Bobby to the Lord and got him baptized in the death cell."

Miers told reporters, "I found Christ not in any hope of escaping the penalty of my crime but in the belief that my example might help others." One of the more cynical reporters later remarked that anyone who believed that story might be interested in buying a bridge in Brooklyn said to be for sale cheap. The press, however, printed the story on front pages all over Texas.

The chaplain, for the benefit of the media, related that Bobby's father had abandoned the family when he was a small child, and he grew up not having a father's guidance and love. Then when his mother was injured in an automobile wreck, Bobby got into trouble and was placed in a reform school. There he met Pegleg Johnson for the first time and was influenced by that older boy. While still teenagers, Bobby and Pegleg escaped from the reform school together. They split up and each separately went on to commit a series of car thefts, robberies, and drug deals.

The chaplain seemed to be saying, in the lyrics of Leonard Bernstein in *West Side Story,* he "was depraved because he was deprived" or perhaps as Hillary says, "His grandmother made him do it."

The press, however, had a feeding frenzy with Bobby's conversion to Christianity. He was photographed in his cell reading the Bible with a soulful look and with a small chain holding a cross draped around his neck. Others chimed into the media circus, and soon "Saving Bobby" became a crusade. Do-gooder groups cited "his unfortunate childhood and teen-age lack of opportunity" as an excuse for his life of crime.

Others made the improbable case that Bobby shot only in self-defense after Sendemer rushed him. The "Save Bobby" crusade gathered state-wide momentum as one San Antonio preacher said of the Hilltop murder, "Society is more guilty than anyone else." At one church, twenty-four-hour, round the clock, "miracle" services were held with large crowds praying for God to save "poor Bobby."

A candlelight vigil of prayer was held one night in the park in front of the Bexar County Courthouse, where hundreds of distressed souls prayed all night for a commutation of the death sentence. Petitions signed by hundreds of voters poured into the office of Texas Governor Allan Shivers, a man who was a shrewd judge of constituency.

In late afternoon on January 8, 1953, Miers, who was scheduled to be electrocuted at midnight, had his head shaved while a clergyman held his hand and prayed aloud. At five o'clock that afternoon a guard brought news. Governor Shivers, in one of his less principled acts, succumbed to political pressure and commuted Miers' sentence to life imprisonment.

At the news, Bobby walked to the wall of his cell and with a smirk tore down the picture of Benjamin Franklin, the father of electricity, taped there. He was not observed to pray.

There was, however, rejoicing among the "crusaders." One preacher opined, "We feel the Lord has won a victory. Had the boy died, it would have been credit for the devil."

During the crocodile tears shed about Miers' unfortunate childhood, the crusaders had perhaps forgotten a small boy who also would not have the love and protection of a father. That was the child of the young man whom Miers had murdered.

CHAPTER 15

Dukes of Duval

For more than sixty years the Parr family, the "Dukes of Duval" controlled four South Texas counties, Jim Wells, Duval, Brooks, and Starr, as if they were feudal monarchs.

The courts, police, county and city officers, and school district officials owed fealty to the family whose control stretched 120 miles from the northern end of Jim Wells County to the southern tip of Starr County bordering on the Rio Grande. The area contained oil fields, cattle ranches, stretches of desert, and fertile farms.

The main Parr stronghold was Duval County. Covering almost 2,000 square miles, it had a population of almost 16,000. Adjacent to the east is Jim Wells County covering 850 square miles with a population of 28,000. The county seat and the largest city in the Parr domain was Alice with more than 20,000 persons. It is, according to *New York Times* reporter Gladwyn Hill, a land of "Cadillacs and coyotes."

Patronage, bribes, and pistoleros, if necessary, kept the population of mostly illiterate Mexican-American field hands voting for Parr candidates. Everybody voted the Parr ticket, both the living and the dead.

As Texas Attorney General John Ben Shepperd charged:

"By controlling elections, you control the sheriff, the district attorney, and county and state district judges. The district judge appoints the grand jury commissioners and they appoint the grand jury. You cannot be arrested, indicted, prosecuted, tried, convicted, or sentenced." It was democracy run amuck.

The first crack in the Parr empire came at the conclusion of World War II when the veterans came home. Uneducated men who had never been fifty miles from home before the war had seen London, Rome, Paris, and Tokyo. Many became the first in their families to attend college, thanks to the G.I. Bill. They were no longer naive field hands who could be herded to the polls or who would quake at the threats of hired pistoleros.

Some small businessmen, lawyers, and civic-minded individuals formed the Freedom Party dedicated to breaking the thralldom imposed by George B. Parr, the current "Duke of Duval." George and his nephew, Archie, reacted violently. While George and Archie alternately held the office of Duval County sheriff, their deputies, hired thugs, wrecked opposition businesses, threatened to withhold welfare checks from impoverished citizens, and resorted to murder to squelch opposition to their empire.

They continued to stuff ballot boxes and fraudulently win local and even state elections. Their most notorious election "fix" was during the 1948 Democratic Party primary for nomination as candidate for the United States Senate. The election pitted Lyndon Johnson against former Governor Coke Stevenson. It was a close and bitter election. Parr supported Johnson.

When the votes were counted election night and the following morning, it appeared that Johnson was ahead. It caused Boss Parr to almost make a fatal mistake. He usually held back election returns from areas he controlled until all other state ballots had been counted. Then he could juggle figures and give his favored candidates the victory. But with Johnson ahead he declared his vote totals before the final count.

But as the final votes across the state were tallied, Johnson's lead evaporated and the Texas Election Bureau announced Stevenson the winner with a 119-vote margin. When this was announced Johnson went into panic. Furious telephone calls went out from Austin to Parr's headquarters. Parr reassured the future president of the United States.

The Duke of Duval informed the election bureau that "corrected" vote totals from Precinct #13 in Alice, Texas, the Jim Wells county seat, gave Johnson an additional 202 votes. That and a few other corrections made Lyndon Johnson the new U.S. Senator from the state of Texas after he trounced a hapless Republican candidate in the November election. Johnson won the nomination with an alleged eighty-seven-vote majority out of over one million votes cast. It gave rise to the derisive nickname "Landslide Lyndon."

Stevenson protested and ordered a probe, but when state investigators and former FBI agents arrived in Alice to examine the "corrected" boxes, they were told that persons unknown had stolen all of them. They were never found, and Johnson took his seat in the U.S. Senate.

In later years George Parr boasted he had engineered the prominence that enabled Johnson to ultimately become president of the United States. If one accepts that boast, without too much extension, one could credit Parr, in addition to the political murders he and his minions committed, with a major contribution to the deaths of 58,000 young Americans during the Vietnam War which was the special provenance of Lyndon Johnson's presidency.

As opposition to his political domination continued to mount despite his threats, Parr's minions became more violent. On July 29, 1949, crusading newspaper editor and radio commentator W.H. (Bill) Mason was shot to death in Alice by Sam Smithwick, a Parr deputy sheriff.

Mason, a fifty-one-year-old veteran journalist, alleged corruption in county construction projects and reported that a Parr-controlled beer joint was also operating as a whorehouse. In response, Smithwick walked up to Mason and in cold blood shot him three times through the heart with a .45-caliber revolver. The deputy felt secure he would be acquitted by a Jim Wells jury on a trumped-up self-defense plea. George would fix things he believed. He was dead wrong.

For once, an uncontrolled grand jury with guts indicted Smithwick for murder. Parr put up $8,000 for the deputy's defense and believed he could fix a jury and arrange an acquittal. He was wrong again. A change of venue was approved by an appointed judge who was not enamored with the Parr machine. Smithwick was tried in straitlaced Bell County in east central Texas more than 200 miles north of Alice. There, a jury of Anglo and German farmers awarded a shocked Smithwick a ninety-nine-year sentence in the state penitentiary in Huntsville.

Mason's murder made the Freedom Party members even more determined in their opposition, but although they grew in strength during the next three years, George Parr was not ready to give up power.

Cracks, however, were beginning to show. On April 15, 1952, Smithwick was found dead in his cell, with a towel tied around his neck, suspended from an upper bunk. It was declared a suicide, but many believed it was a murder engineered by Parr to keep a disillusioned deputy from talking about Parr illegalities in exchange for a lightened sentence.

On the evening of September 8, 1952, Jacob "Jake" Floyd, an Alice attorney and a pillar of strength in the Freedom Party, received an urgent telephone call from Nago Alaniz, a local lawyer, requesting an immediate and secret meeting. Jake told his twenty-one-year-old son Jake Jr. "Buddy" Floyd that he was going to a meeting at the Jewel Drive-In.

When he met Alaniz, the lawyer told Floyd that Parr planned to have him killed. Two pistoleros had been hired to gun him down and he, Alaniz, had been ordered to furnish the two with an alibi.

Alaniz confided that the leader of the killers was Mario "The Turk" Sapet, a special deputy sheriff of Duval County. The trigger-man was a Mexican gunman named Alfredo Cervantes. Alarmed, Jake headed for home. He was too late.

Buddy, worried about his dad, told his fiancée that he was going to the drive-in. "I'll be back soon," he said. As he was leaving the house, a dark green Packard automobile, lights dimmed, pulled up near the Floyd home. The Turk was driving with Cervantes beside him. They stopped the car and Cervantes eased out of the front seat of the car at the same instant Buddy came out of the house. In the dark, Cervantes thought it was Jake.

The gunman fired four shots from a .38-caliber automatic pistol as Buddy stepped onto the driveway. One struck the young man in the hand, another in the head. Cervantes ran back to the Packard, and the two sped toward the border bridge at Nuevo Laredo and safety in Mexico at ninety miles per hour.

Just as the Packard sped off, Buddy's mother drove up to the driveway. When her headlights revealed a sprawled body, she rushed from the car screaming "Buddy, Buddy" as she recognized her son lying on the drive with blood pouring from his head. Almost simultaneously, Jake arrived. The rushed their son to the Alice hospital, but he died eighteen hours later.

Infuriated Texas Rangers turned Alice upside down, not without results. They found the murder weapon in a trashcan where Cervantes had stupidly dumped it. From its serial numbers they traced it to the Turk, who foolishly had returned to San Antonio where he was arrested.

Cervantes, however, found a safe haven in Mexico. Connected with high officials in the state government and the Mexican Federal Police, he was able to block all legal efforts to extradite him for trial in Texas. But the trigger-man was embittered. Because he had murdered the wrong man, carelessly thrown away the murder weapon, which caused Sapet's arrest, and created more ranger heat on Parr, the Duke refused to pay the bungling pistolero.

Desperate for justice, the members of the Freedom Party turned to Johnny Klevenhagen. Someone had to go into Mexico, locate Cervantes, take him into custody (kidnap him), and haul him across the border where he would face Texas justice. The best candidates for the job were Texas Rangers. Both Captain Alfred Allee and his sidekick, Ranger Joe Bridge, who were assigned to South Texas, were notoriously well known south of the Rio Grande; as was Ranger Zeno Smith, who was then headquartered in San Antonio. But Floyd and his friends recognized that the greatest manhunter of them all was a ranger named Johnny Klevenhagen. Johnny, they believed, could bring in Cervantes.

Throughout the previous one hundred years, the Texas Rangers had treated the Texas-Mexican border barriers less than casually. It was an attitude born of necessity rather than arrogance because it was regretfully known that a Mexican criminal, if he had money or political connections, could never be extradited. Consequently, over the years the rangers would deal with cross-border rustlers, robbers, and murderers in ways other than official. An example of ranger justice, whispered around police circles and newspaper press rooms, concerned Ranger Zeno Smith.

It began in July 1953, when a burning automobile was found on a desolate stretch of a Duval County road. In it was the body of a U.S. Border Patrol officer who had been shot to death. The officer was known to be hostile to Parr interests and had been conducting an investigation into the border boss' affairs.

Through informers, rangers learned the identity of the killer, a hired pistolero who had fled into Mexico. It was rumored that Parr hired the killer, and the murder became something of a joke in some barrooms in Nuevo Laredo. The killer, confident he was untouchable, when full of tequila, was known to boast of killing an American lawman. However, he may have made one fatal miscalculation; the murdered border patrolman had been a close friend of Texas Ranger Zeno Smith.

Zeno was a ranger of the old school. Pushing sixty, he was of medium height, large girth, and with his snow-white hair resembled a jovial Santa Claus. He was a man who talked much but really said little. In cases he solved he always gave credit to local police and deputies and minimized his role. He smiled often, but not with his eyes. For years he scared the hell out of criminals in the San Antonio area of his jurisdiction.

The author recalls one summer afternoon after the border patrolman's murder when Zeno sauntered into the pressroom of the San Antonio Police Department headquarters. "Well boys," he said, "I'm going to take a little vacation. I may visit some of my friends down in old Mexico." With that, he sauntered out.

Several weeks later he returned to the pressroom saying, "Well boys, I'm back from my vacation." The author queried, "Say Zeno, did they ever catch the pistolero that murdered that border patrolman down in Duval?" Zeno smiled but his eyes were cold. "That case is cleared," he said, and he turned on his boot heels and stalked out of the room. The pistolero was never seen again.

Back in Alice a collection was taken up to defer expenses for a trip into Mexico by Johnny and a Mexican-American detective on the San Antonio police force who knew Cervantes by sight. They had no lethal intent. They planned to accost Cervantes and make him an offer to return to Texas and face a fair trial. It would be an offer he couldn't refuse. And most important, if Cervantes was convicted, to save himself from "Old Sparky," the Huntsville prison's electric chair, he might implicate Parr as the man who ordered the murder of Jake Floyd.

The two American lawmen had received information about the location of Cervantes' hideout in the Nuevo Leon desert. Dressed in the clothing of peasant farm workers, the two purchased a supply of tortillas, beans, and coffee, filled canteens, loaded up their backpacks, and slipped into the desert wilderness at nightfall.

Hiking through the barren countryside, they made camp on a small hillside overlooking the hideout. They were hardly happy campers. There were rattlesnakes and the ubiquitous and vicious Mexican stinging scorpions, and almost every plant that grew had sharp and stinging spines.

For more than a week they suffered the blowing dust, the burning daytime heat, and the nighttime chill of the desert climate. Johnny's eyes ached and burned from spending hours watching Cervantes' house through binoculars, but there was no sign of the gunman.

Finally as supplies and patience had about given out and the canteens were running dry, Johnny spotted a plume of dust in the distance coming down the dirt road leading to the house. Cocking their weapons, the lawmen waited until the automobile pulled up in front of the house and three men got out.

"That's Cervantes," the detective said, pointing to one of the men. "Let's go," Johnny replied, and the two men, weapons drawn, ran down the hill and confronted the trio. As the three men, hands held high in the air, glared at the Americans, the detective said, "Damn. I made a mistake, that's not him." Johnny's response was an expletive.

There was nothing to do but get the hell out. Weapons at the ready, the two lawmen backed up, then ran back up the hill and back into the desert followed by curses and threats from the three Mexicans.

Their cover blown, the lawmen knew they had to get out of Mexico, fast. The alarm would be spread, and soon an enraged posse of pistoleros and Mexican Federal Police—the two were virtually indistinguishable—would be on their trail. If they were caught, they knew their fate. Their bodies would be left on the desert as supper for coyotes.

Making their way to the first village with a telephone, they put in a desperate call to their Freedom Party friends in Alice. "Get us out of here, quick," they implored. A rendezvous was arranged, and the two hid out until twilight when a light airplane landed on a secluded dirt road. Klevenhagen and the detective leaped into it and breathed a sigh of relief only when they cleared Mexican airspace and landed at the Alice airport. It had been a good try. They failed but at least they were alive.

The Freedom Party went into a funk after the failed attempt. Again, it seemed, Parr had had someone murdered and gotten away with it. Justice long delayed, however, would not be forever denied.

The outrage over the Buddy Floyd murder resulted in Texas Governor Allan Shivers and Attorney General Price Daniel launching a massive investigation into Parr's corrupt empire. Shivers ordered in the Texas Rangers to keep the peace and protect Parr's political opponents. The job was given to Ranger Captain Alfred Allee, who not only hated Parr's guts but who was, in the opinion of many, the toughest ranger to ever pin on the Ranger badge.

Allee, near retirement, was elderly and of less than medium height, but he possessed a deadly aura, a not rare attribute of old-time rangers. Historian and historical novelist David Nevin in his book *The Texans* explained it best.

"A Ranger," Nevin wrote, "has a capacity not just to command but to dominate...by some inner force....It really has nothing to do with size or toughness or strength, and these are truly dangerous men....It is deep, primeval." Such a man was Alfred Allee, bushy-browed, cigar-chomping, and with a temper that was as quick as his fists.

The aging captain was the one man feared by Parr's pistolero deputies. Among the people of Duval and Jim Wells Counties, he was, if not loved, greatly respected. The author recalls the captain walking softly down the streets of Alice during the times when Parr was under investigation. The predominant Mexican-American population of farm workers upon encountering him would doff their hats and smiling say, "Buenos dias, el Capitan Allee." Parr's men would cross the street to keep the hell out of his way. When greeted, the captain would touch the brim of his Stetson, nod, and continue his one-man parade down the dusty avenues.

Allee usually had only one or two other rangers from his Company D to aid him. As *New York Times* reporter Gladwyn Hill wrote, "The detachment never numbered more than two or three men at a time, one Texas Ranger traditionally being the equivalent of a brigade of ordinary peace officers."

In much of South Texas, fear was a constant companion and Hill reported, "Be-pistoled Texas Rangers walked the streets of Alice and nearby communities. Inhabitants eyed each other nervously and started at the backfire of automobiles." The fear has never completely gone away. Almost fifty years later when the author questioned a man prominent in Duval County affairs about the Floyd killing, he replied, "You don't talk about those things here. They'll kill your children."

While Allee and Ranger Joe Bridge prevented violence in Duval and Jim Wells Counties, by the fall of 1952 a team of accountants and lawyers from the attorney general's office began to put the area under an investigative microscope. Before long the FBI and the Bureau of Internal Revenue lent their ominous presence to the probe.

In March 1954 a political opponent charged that Parr threatened him with a pistol. Brought to court on this charge, both Archie and George made the almost fatal mistake of bad-mouthing Texas Rangers. In the courthouse corridor, Archie Parr, who had succeeded his uncle as sheriff of Duval County, made a slurring remark to Ranger Bridge. For that bit of foolish bravado he got a slap in the face that sent his glasses flying and dumped his rear on the courthouse floor. Archie drew his revolver.

Allee, paunchy, old, and not in the best of health, reacted like a startled rattler. With one hand he drew his pistol and with the other he twisted the gun out of Archie's hand. George Parr leaped to attack the old ranger, but Allee spun around, grabbed the Duke's ear, and twisting, practically tore it off. He grabbed the Duke's pistol and threw it to the floor. Red faced and boiling mad, he was about to kill when a young lady newspaper reporter, Caro Brown, leaped between the two men shouting, "Don't do it, Captain. Please don't. Please don't." Allee slowly regained his composure. Everyone, including Parr, who limped off with his ear streaming blood, agreed she saved the fifty-two-year-old tyrant's life. Many thought Caro's act was brave but wished she had been elsewhere. Parr was fined $150 for rudely displaying a firearm. He later filed civil rights charges against Allee and Bridges, which were dismissed.

Later Parr and many of his henchmen were tried and convicted of mail fraud and theft and sentenced to long terms in prison. Mario "The Turk" Sapet was tried in a North Texas court and luckily escaped the death penalty but received a ninety-nine-year sentence in state prison. Parr was brought to trial on additional charges of stealing money from the Benavides Independent School District. He was tried and convicted and sentenced to five years in prison.

In July 1957 Parr was tried in federal court on mail fraud charges. He was defended by famed attorney Percy Foreman, who specialized in getting murderers and other assorted villains off the hook with tactics of flamboyance, bluster, and buffoonery which managed to flummox semiliterate East Texas jurors. It didn't work for Parr, and the Duke received a ten-year prison sentence. As the judge announced the verdict, Parr looked panic-stricken and Percy was visibly upset by his failure. Johnny, who was present, sat there grinning. It didn't quite make up for the Mexican fiasco, but it helped.

In later years constant pressure by Texas authorities resulted in Cervantes being prosecuted for murder in a Mexico City court where he was convicted and sent to prison. How much time he actually spent in jail is not known.

Parr, slippery as ever, had all of his convictions dismissed in appeals courts. In 1974, however, he was again convicted of income tax evasion. It was a charge he could not get reversed. On April 1, 1975, he got into his prized Chrysler automobile and drove out across his ranch until he came to a clearing near a windmill and a concrete water tank where he stopped the car. He left the engine running, then he took out his .45-caliber automatic pistol, pressed it to the right side of his head, squeezed the trigger, and blew out his brains. The Duke of Duval was dead, and an era of South Texas history had ended.

CHAPTER 16

Cop Killer

State Highway Patrolman Robert James Crosby and his partner Doyce C. Doolin were enjoying a quiet Saturday night on November 27, 1954, as they patrolled along the Beaumont highway leading out of Houston. The window was down and a soft, cool breeze drifting through the car was particularly pleasant after months of the hellish Gulf Coast summer weather. Their reverie came to a quick end when a 1946 black Chevrolet roared past them doing eighty miles an hour.

"Here we go again," Crosby grinned, as he sped in pursuit. As both cars raced through the blackness of a moonless night a thickening fog rolled in from the south further hampering visibility, and soon the speeder's taillights began to recede into the darkness. They passed several side roads barely visible in the gloom and then topping a small rise, the taillights were no longer in sight. "He must have turned off on one of those side roads," Doolin said.

They doubled back and searched side roads and dead ends until they were back in the Houston city limits but had no luck. In disgust they gave up the chase. "You can't win them all," Crosby muttered as they continued their patrolling.

About 9:00 P.M. Harris County Deputy Sheriff Jimmy Scarborough left his home at Jacinto City to work the night shift at the Houston headquarters. He hauled his motorcycle out of the garage, kicked the kickstand up, and straddling the big Harley drove south on the Beaumont highway. Reveling in the cool breeze, he was cruising along when he heard the screech of brakes behind him. A black Chevy had almost run him down.

Scarborough inwardly cursed motorists who couldn't or wouldn't see motorcycles until they were right on top of them. The deputy continued on, but within a few seconds it happened again: the screeching of brakes and the Chevy pulling up only a few feet behind him.

Annoyed with this idiot driver, Scarborough pulled over to the side of the road as he was crossing the bridge over Hunting Bayou and waved the driver to pass him. The Chevy pulled around him swinging wildly across the road as it passed. As the car sped ahead, the deputy saw it swerve across the road and force two automobiles to run onto the shoulder to avoid a collision.

"Damn drunk," Scarborough snarled as he turned on his flashing red light and siren and sped into pursuit. At a point about a mile north of the intersection of U.S. Highway 73 and the Beaumont highway, he pulled up alongside the speeding auto and motioned the driver to pull over. The driver nodded, hit his brakes, and slid to a stop on the shoulder.

Scarborough pulled up behind the car, got off the cycle, and strode over to the Chevy on the driver's side. Walking up to the auto, the deputy observed the driver was in his early thirties with an unshaved face and a cold stare. Sitting beside him appeared to be a visibly nervous teenager.

Assuming the driver was drunk, Scarborough said, "Say friend, you've driven about far enough for the condition you're in."

The driver didn't answer but opened the door and stepped out into the street. As he did, the deputy caught the glint of a nickel-plated .38-caliber revolver, then there was a searing pain in his right arm, and the roar of a pistol shot shocked his ears.

The force of the bullet knocked the deputy backward, and he stumbled and fell behind the car. The shooter, without saying a word or changing his bland expression, calmly got back into the Chevy and drove off.

Fortunately the bullet missed bone, and although it hurt like hell, Scarborough pulled his .45 automatic and sent off a volley of shots at the fleeing driver. As he lay on the roadside, a following motorist stopped and rushed to the officer's side.

Seeing the bleeding arm, the motorist said, "My God, let me take you to the hospital." Scarborough refused, "Hell no, help me into your car and let's take after those guys." Only after a fruitless pursuit in which they lost sight of the Chevy did the deputy consent to being driven to the emergency ward of the Galena Park Hospital. Scarborough put out an all-points bulletin on the automobile and its two occupants, let the emergency room doctor bandage where the bullet went in and out, called someone to pick up his motorcycle, and then hitched a ride to the sheriff's office.

Meanwhile Crosby and Doolin were back cruising along McCarty Avenue unaware of Scarborough's shooting when they again saw the black Chevy. This time it was coming straight at them at a blazing rate of speed. As the auto raced by them, Crosby grinned, "We've got 'em again," made a tire shrieking, 180-degree turn, and took up pursuit. Within a few moments they overtook the Chevy and forced it off the road against an embankment where both cars came to an abrupt stop.

As Doolin stepped out of the police car, he was met by a shotgun blast that momentarily staggered him as a buckshot pellet ripped open his cheek. Falling back behind his auto, he drew his revolver and opened fire. He saw Crosby, trying to get out of the car, stagger again and again under a rain of double aught buckshot and .30-30 rifle bullets. The barrage from the Chevy blew out the patrol car's windshield and peppered the interior with flying lead. As the fusillade of gunshots shattered the still of the autumn night, both automobiles were turned into undrivable wrecks.

As Doolin reloaded he heard a cursing voice yell, "The damn rifle's jammed. I can't get the lever to work. We got to get the hell outta here." Then the two men dashed from their auto, ran into the brush by the side of the road, and vanished into the night.

With blood pouring from his ripped cheek, Doolin forced open the door of the shattered patrol car. Crosby was slumped dying across the steering wheel. Doolin got on the radio and gave that most feared cry, "Officer down. Badly wounded; send help." Then he gave their location. During the seemingly interminable few minutes until a dozen siren-screaming police cars and an ambulance arrived, Doolin stroked his partner's hand and prayed.

While the twenty-seven-year-old officer's life was draining away, thirty-two-year-old Merle Ellisor and his twenty-year-old brother Archie were running through high weeds and brambles in an effort to escape. Suddenly Merle stumbled and gasped, "Sonny, I am hit bad. We got to stop somewhere." But he quickly recovered, and the two men ran almost a mile across an open field to a pipe yard off McCarty Avenue. There, with the strength of desperation they scaled a ten-foot fence, ripping their hands on the three strands of barbed wire at the top, and dropped into the pipe yard.

Merle, feeling faint and bleeding steadily, said, "Archie, I've gone as far as I can go. I'm going to crawl into these big pipes. You got to go get a car and come back for me. I'll meet you on the road." Then he crawled toward a stand of large-diameter pipe.

Archie climbed back over the fence and walked down McCarty Avenue until he hailed a passing taxicab, which he had take him to the home of his brother-in-law. There, he told his sister and her husband, "Merle is in trouble and he's hurt bad. I need your car." The brother-in-law reluctantly turned over his car keys, and Archie drove back to the pipe yard. He circled the area again and again, but there was no sign of Merle. Frightened when the whole area came alive with police cars, he panicked and drove off.

At the Klevenhagen home, Johnny, Viola, and John Jr. were spending a quiet evening when ominously the telephone rang and Johnny soon heard the news of the wounded officer. Soon he joined more than fifty state, county, and city police officers at the McCarty Road site. Inspecting the two shot-up automobiles, he spotted a twelve-gauge shotgun and the jammed .30-30 deer rifle lying on the ground by the Chevy.

Within the hour bloodhounds from the state prison farm were sniffing around the underbrush trying to pick up a scent from bloodstains on the grass.

Earlier, when Crosby lay dying, an ambulance arrived, followed by a physician motorist who stopped his automobile and got out to render aid. As they loaded Crosby into the ambulance the physician got in and continued to render first aid. But it was to no avail as the officer died on the way to the hospital. There, Crosby was placed in a holding room for a short time and then his body was taken to a funeral home.

Meanwhile, Jo Evelyn Crosby, after being notified her husband had been wounded, rushed to the hospital only to find he was dead and the body had been removed. On learning this, the young wife became hysterical. She was given a sedative and, ironically, placed in bed in the same room in which her husband's body had been kept.

By this time, scores of police officers were scouting the area including the indefatigable Officer Doolin, who with a bandaged cheek insisted on helping Johnny organize part of the search.

It was close to midnight when Archie, still in a high state of panic, returned to his brother-in-law's house where in addition to his sister he was joined by his wife and his two small children. When he told them he must go back and look for Merle, the two women raised loud vocal objections until Archie relented saying, "I've got to get out of town."

At this, brother-in-law, sister, wife, two children, and Archie piled into their automobile and drove twenty-five miles until they reached the small town of Liberty. There they dropped Archie off at Keller's Tourist Court where he rented a room and soon fell into a troubled and exhausted sleep.

The police tracing the shot-up killer's automobile put out a dragnet for all known friends and relatives of the Ellisor brothers. When Archie's tired and terrified family finally reached home around four o'clock Sunday morning and pulled into their driveway, they were startled when suddenly blinding lights lit up the area as half a dozen grim-faced police officers surrounded the car, pointing everything from shotguns to submachine guns in their faces.

After the two kids were put to bed, Johnny had a discussion with the remaining family members. Within a few minutes he made several telephone calls. He turned to his fellow officers and said, "Archie is in Liberty. I've notified the local police. Let's go." It is not officially known who gave away Archie's whereabouts, but beyond a doubt a hard-faced Ranger Klevenhagen made pointed remarks about the pleasantries of the Texas penal system while mentioning the penalties for aiding and abetting a man wanted for murdering a police officer. In any event, within moments a caravan of lawmen, heavily armed, drove at high speed for the Liberty motel.

At 6:30 Sunday morning young Archie's troubled sleep came to an end when the door of his room burst open and Johnny, gun in hand, followed by a dozen angry lawmen, loomed over his bed.

A slender, dark, wavy-haired young man, Archie looked down the barrels of the drawn guns and swore he had not shot at anyone. "My brother, Merle, he's an ex-con, he did the shooting," Archie pleaded. Pulled from bed, he was pushed into the back of a patrol car and driven back to the scene of Officer Crosby's murder.

Archie yammered to Johnny, "When we were running away from the car, Merle handed me his pistol. I took it and then threw it away as far as I could. I don't know where it went." As Archie was hauled off to the county jail, Johnny organized a large posse of police and volunteer civilians to beat the underbrush searching for both Merle and the thrown away pistol that was used to shoot Deputy Scarborough.

There was thick dry brush, tall weeds, stagnant pools of water, and not a few cottonmouths and rattlesnakes in the open fields nearby. To both protect the searchers and help clear the area and possibly to smoke out Merle, Johnny called the Fire Department and, after a brief conference with the district chief, checked the wind direction and then supervised the setting of a wide brush fire. As police rerouted traffic and fire trucks stood by, a long line of searchers, close enough to join hands with each other, slowly tromped behind a scorching fire of dry grass and weeds and clouds of black smoke, but neither the killer nor his weapon was found.

They did find a light brown suede jacket, with a bullet hole in the back of the garment, draped over a pair of shoes, which Archie identified as belonging to his brother.

Searching through police records, Johnny found that Merle, at age thirty-two, had a long record as a criminal. In March 1948 he had been shot in the liver and lung by Houston homicide detective R.D. Langdon while attempting to escape from the city jail. In November of that year, after recovering from the gunshot wounds, he was tried, convicted, and sentenced to a long period in the state penitentiary for felony theft. But in May of the following year he escaped from prison and returned to Houston where he remained at large. Young brother Archie had no criminal record.

The lawmen and volunteers spent all day Sunday and Monday scouring the area around the pipe yard. After seventy-two hours of fruitless effort the exhausted police received a new clue. An eighteen-year-old student told police he had picked up a hitchhiker Sunday night in an area near the fatal shooting. The hitchhiker was barefoot and his feet were blackened with mud. He told the student he had gotten drunk and was "rolled for most of my money." But he said he had five dollars in quarters and would pay if the student would take him to a Houston area, which turned out to be in a neighborhood where he had relatives. The student agreed. The following Monday when he saw Merle's photograph on the front pages of the local newspapers, he recognized him as the man he had ferried on Saturday night and hurried to tell his story to police.

At this time Johnny received information that earlier in the week a burglary of a Houston business office was reported in which a deer rifle, shotgun, and .38-caliber pistol were stolen as well as $130 in cash, $31 of which were in quarters. Then he received a report that two tugboats tied up in Bray's Bayou had been robbed of blankets, shirts, khaki pants, two pairs of brown shoes, a tarpaulin, and a few cans of food.

A sleepless, weary-eyed Klevenhagen told reporters he believed Merle Ellisor was the thief and that he was probably planning to camp out until the heat died down. As he began to assemble another search party, he had a number of Merle's relations given lie detector tests; however, they shed no light on the killer's hiding place.

Doggedly, Klevenhagen and local officers took up the search in the rough areas around Bray's Bayou until about 10:30 Wednesday morning when two Houston policemen spotted Merle dozing on a bed of newspapers spread in high weeds. Covering him with their shotguns, they bid him an unpleasant good morning, handcuffed him, and brought him to the city jail. He had been hiding out for more than eighty hours; he was bearded, exhausted, hungry, and had a policeman's bullet embedded in his back. "I'm Merle Ellisor and you've got me," he groaned to the jailers. He had three pennies and $26 in quarters in his pockets.

He was taken to the hospital where the bullet was removed. He was later returned to the police station where he told a cold-blooded story of burglary and murder. Speaking deadpan and using crude grammar, Merle recounted that after stealing the three weapons, on Saturday afternoon the two brothers and other relatives "had a sort of a picnic." They drove out into the countryside, and after an impromptu shooting match, they enjoyed a round of sandwiches and beer.

When Johnny asked Merle why he shot the three police officers, he muttered, "It just happened. I can't explain it. I was scared. . . . I don't know. I was just drunk."

Ironically, during Merle's statement to police officers and newspaper reporters, Detective Langdon, who had shot him during his attempted escape from the Houston jail in 1948, walked up and smiling said, "Do you remember me, Merle?" Ellisor looked up, rubbed his hand across his chest, and grunted, "Yeah."

That Saturday night, after the picnic, Merle related that he and Archie got into their auto and were speeding down the Beaumont Highway "because I was in a hurry for a date with a barmaid." It was his speeding car that caught the eyes of Patrolmen Crosby and Doolin and later Deputy Scarborough and set in motion the tragic train of events that led to Officer Crosby's death.

After eighty-four hours without sleep and sustained only by countless cups of black coffee, an exhausted Johnny Klevenhagen went home and collapsed into bed. The strain of such cases was to result in grim consequences to the ranger's health.

In the subsequent trial, Merle was convicted of murder and sentenced to die in the electric chair for killing Officer Crosby and Archie was sentenced to state prison for burglary.

On the evening of April 4, 1957, Merle Ellisor sat in the death cell at Huntsville State Prison where he had spent the past seventeen months. There he learned his last appeals for clemency had been refused and he was to die that night. That evening Archie, also imprisoned in Huntsville, was granted a last visit with his older brother. A prison guard later said the two joked with each other and seemed unconcerned with Merle's date with "Old Sparky."

Merle's demeanor changed when Archie left and one of his sisters came to say good-bye. Then, as they held each other, both broke down and cried.

Visitations over, Merle ate a last meal of oysters and fried shrimp. Then his head and legs were shaved and his pants leg slit. When the guards came, he said, "I'm ready to go. I've been ready for a long time."

Then he began the walk down the corridor toward the small enclosed room where a heavily wired chair awaited him. He smiled as he passed a cell where a cut-out magazine picture of Benjamin Franklin was taped to the wall. The grim humor of the condemned block honored old Ben as the father of electricity.

One of the condemned jauntily shouting, "Merle, don't sit down," brought a weak grin to his strained face. He was taken to the site of "The Chair," strapped in, and as a lever was pulled and jail lights momentarily dimmed, his body strained mightily, his bowels released, there was a smell of burnt hair, and Merle Ellisor paid the final price for murdering a young police officer.

CHAPTER 17

Norris—The Smiling Killer

He looked just like the boy next door. Slender, with light, wavy, chestnut-brown hair, soft blue eyes, and an ingratiating smile. He seemed a very pleasant and polite young man. Looks, however, deceived, for Gene Paul Norris was a psychopathic, cold-blooded killer whose like had not been seen in Texas since the days of John Wesley Hardin.

Police believed he murdered more than forty men, and his terrible tally might have gone higher if he had taken the advice of Johnny Klevenhagen. But he didn't and it was a career ending mistake.

Norris never received the notoriety that lofted Hardin, Baby Face Nelson, Bonnie and Clyde, Pretty Boy Floyd, and other murderers into the ranks of motion picture legend. It is just as well for he deserves to be forgotten. As for his good manners, Samuel Johnson's description of Lord Chesterfield seems appropriate, "He has the morals of a whore and the manners of a dancing master," although the comparison is probably too hard on whores.

Perhaps he first learned to hate back in 1937 when he was fifteen years old. At that time his older brother, Thomas

Nathan (Pete) Norris, then only twenty-one years old, made the top of the list as Public Enemy #1 in Texas and Oklahoma. Finally caught by Texas police, Pete was sentenced to ninety-nine years in prison for murdering a bookie. He was convicted mainly on the testimony of a Houston gambler and bookie named Johnnie Brannan, a man who both brothers swore to kill at the first opportunity.

During his lifetime, Gene was arrested twenty-five times and sent to prison six times. As a teenager his first arrests were for forgery, but he quickly turned to more brutal crimes. While still a minor he was acquitted of armed robbery of a food market. Following the outbreak of World War II he was arrested for draft evasion, but he broke out of the Conroe City Jail and began raising hell all over Texas.

On March 16, 1942, when Gene was twenty years old, he engineered a daring daylight jailbreak at Ferguson State Prison, located six miles from the small East Texas town of Midway. Norris had learned that his now twenty-six-year-old brother, Pete, who was skilled in carpentry, was working on the construction of a new home for the manager of the prison's farm.

Gene and a friend stole a large 1941 Plymouth sedan and headed for Ferguson. When they passed Midway they stopped and Gene shinnied up the telephone pole whose line connected with the prison. Laughing, he clipped all the wires, cutting off the prison from the outside world. Then they drove to the farm manager's house where seven prisoners, including Pete, were working, watched by two guards with rifles.

As they drove up to the house and stopped, Gene smiled at the guards, stepped out of the auto, and shoved an automatic pistol in their faces. Still smiling, he politely said,

"Please stick 'em up." The astonished guards dropped their rifles and stuck 'em up. They were quickly tied up.

Then Pete and six other hardened convicts piled into the crammed Plymouth and sped north. After traveling thirty-five miles, near the small town of Buffalo, they abandoned the Plymouth. After stealing two more automobiles they split up. Five of the prisoners, all in one auto, headed south toward Houston, but they were caught three days later at a roadblock near LaGrange. Gene, his accomplice, Pete, and another prisoner headed northwest for Dallas, but they eluded police for only a few days more.

Presumably afraid that Pete would outlive his ninety-nine-year sentence, authorities tried him for the escape and additional crimes and sentenced him to 400 additional years in state prison. He would be given no more outside carpentry jobs. For engineering the escape and draft dodging, perhaps because of his youth, Gene received only an eight-year sentence. The leniency was a mistake.

Pete was a restive prisoner, and on February 27, 1945, he and a fellow convict escaped from Retrieve Prison Farm and made their way to Detroit before being recaptured by the FBI. For reasons known only to government bureaucrats, not satisfied with the 499 years of prison sentences already amassed against him, Pete was brought to Wharton, Texas, where he was tried for jail-breaking, convicted, and had ten more years tacked onto his half millennium prison tour.

On Christmas Eve his lawyer telephoned him. Pete was released from his cell to take the call but unbeknownst to his jailers had a cheap Saturday Night Special revolver that somehow had been smuggled into his cell. When he reached the telephone in the sheriff's office, he pulled the pistol out of his pocket, pointed it at the half dozen lawmen present, and with a grin said, "Stick 'em up, fellas."

Sheriff "Buckshot" Lane of Wharton County was a slender man of unprepossessing size, but it was said, "If riled, he would charge Godzilla." He charged Pete.

With a flying tackle Lane knocked Norris to the floor. Falling, Norris fired, and the bullet went whizzing past Lane's ear. It was the only shot he got off as Lane rolled away and his deputies opened fire. Before the melee was finished, Pete was shot in the left shoulder and right chest, and the middle finger of his right hand was blown off. After he recovered it was said he pledged to become a model prisoner for the remainder of his 509-year sentence.

Baby brother Gene was released from prison in 1950. According to police intelligence, the young man hired out as a paid assassin for whoever was willing to bankroll a murder. Most of his estimated forty victims were underworld characters. Using his favorite weapon, a sawed-off twelve-gauge shotgun, he retired, with prejudice, a growing number of gamblers, dope peddlers, stool pigeons, and other criminals who had crossed or betrayed other crooks more lethal than they. A romantic touch to his string of murders was when he shot to death one Cecil Green, who was the husband of the woman who quickly became his wife.

In April 1953 he was acquitted of staging a robbery of two exiled Cuban gunrunners at Houston's Western Hills Motel, during which time he relieved them of $248,000. He was soon back in jail on other charges until he was again released from prison in 1955.

It was about this time that Gene Norris drifted back to Houston. He was staying at an expensive motel when there was a knock on his door. Opening it, he saw a tall, hard-faced man in Stetson and boots standing before him. "I'm Johnny Klevenhagen," the man said.

Norris smiled, "I know who you are. Come in and sit down." So face to face, the worst killer since John Wesley

Captain Klevenhagen is wearing his favorite Stetson
in this 1956 photograph.

Hardin and one of the toughest Texas Rangers ever sat across from one another for a brief conversation.

"You are not wanted now," Klevenhagen said, "but if there are any shotgunnings around here, I'll be coming after you. Get out of town and stay out." The ranger rose and went to the door.

Norris, still smiling, said, "I just came down here to visit my brother in jail. Now, I'm leaving. My business here is finished." The brief meeting ended. Norris, however, was lying. It was a mistake.

Gene didn't leave but instead hid out with friends. Soon he boasted he would gun down Klevenhagen if the ranger ever dared to try and arrest him. He frequently complained, "The police are always hounding me. They no longer consider me a member of the human race." Altogether it was a rather accurate judgement.

It wasn't long before Houston police, through informers, learned there had been a series of armed robberies of gamblers, dope sellers, and pimps which was followed up by a daring holdup of a gambling casino. In each case the robbers were two men armed with shotguns.

In March a well-known gambler was held up and robbed of several hundred dollars and a pistol. In April the two shotgun wielders entered a gambling club in Dickinson, held the owners and guests at gunpoint, and made off with $28,000 in cash. Houston police were hearing increasing rumors of stickups, and in some cases a few underworld characters simply disappeared, never to be seen again.

It was obviously part of a plan. Those hit were always on the shady side of the law or were outright criminals who could not or would not make reports to the police. To Johnny it had the smell of Gene Paul Norris. And the deadly hand of the smiling killer became apparent when his twenty-year-old threat to murder Houston gambler John Brannan seemed fulfilled in a most grisly manner.

On the morning of April 17, a gambler who worked for Brannan called him on the telephone and got no answer. After repeated calls received no response, the gambler became suspicious and called the police. When a patrol car pulled up in front of Brannan's house and the officers rang the doorbell, there was only silence from inside. Trying the door, they found it unlocked.

Upon entering the house they found fifty-nine-year-old Brannan and his fifty-seven-year-old wife, Lillie, dead with their skulls smashed in and their faces butchered. The murder weapon, according to police pathologists, was probably an axe or a hatchet wielded with great force. Brannan was found lying on his stomach in the front bedroom wearing red-striped pajamas. His hands were taped behind his back and he was gagged with a red bandanna. The force of the blows had popped his left eye out of its socket and broken his neck.

Lillie's body was in the back bedroom. She was seated in a rocking chair wearing a simple print dress and a towel was thrown over her battered head. Her neck was also broken from the force of the blows to her head.

When Klevenhagen arrived on the scene, he talked to neighbors who told him they saw a green 1957 Chevrolet parked in front of the Brannan's house about ten o'clock that morning. From other evidence found in the house, the ranger constructed a grim scenario. He believed two men in a green automobile showed up that morning and rang the doorbell, and when Brannan opened the door they greeted him at gunpoint. There was no sign of forced entry. Blood on towels and splattered on the bathroom sink indicated that after slaughtering their victims the men washed the blood off their hands and then went into the kitchen.

Lillie had earlier made a pot of coffee, and the two killers helped themselves to a refreshing cup as was evidenced by two used coffee cups on the table. A police forensic expert found smudged fingerprints and deduced that one of the murder weapons was wielded by a left-handed man.

The house was ransacked. Brannan's wallet was found emptied, and in the covered garage, the gambler's Cadillac was found with the trunk opened. The more than a dozen bookies who worked for Brannan later told police that their boss made a daily collection from his horse race bets and numbers racket operations that netted him more than $5,000. The money, they said, was always put into the trunk compartment of the Cadillac. While Klevenhagen smelled the cold-blooded butchery as the work of Norris, the Houston police had a series of red herrings strewn in their path.

Lillie's sister told police that Lillie had been recently worried by persons calling her husband on the telephone and others coming to their door asking for loans, saying they were desperate for money. Most lawmen dismissed this as the occupational hazard of a big-time horse race bookie as the perennial losers are always begging for loans and credit.

Although Brannan possessed a federal gambling license and had in past years been arrested eleven times for gambling offenses, he had no record of being involved in violence. Neighbors said the couple had no known enemies and that he always appeared dressed in a businessman's suit and tie. His wife, who had had three operations for throat cancer, was active in church work. They were, it was said, a pleasant, friendly, and devoted couple. Not quite.

Klevenhagen located a good-looking waitress who told him she was "Big John's mistress for twenty years." The girlfriend, who probably knew more about Brannan's business than the wife, told the ranger that it was well known that Brannan carried more than $5,000 in cash in his pockets. She said she had seen him the day before he was murdered and he was relaxed and joking. He was a kind man, she said, and had no known enemies.

Since Brannan's gambling activities extended through both Harris and nearby Ft. Bend Counties, local police rounded up all known bookies in the two-county area. Soon the sheriff's offices looked like a scene from Damon Runyon's *Guys and Dolls*. And many of the gamblers were scared stiff. Some of them readily admitted that they had recently been held up at gunpoint, and others were afraid they would be next on a hit list.

Some of the gamblers believed a rival gangland syndicate was trying to muscle into Brannan's territory. On a tip that three gamblers associated with Brannan were headed for Mexico in a green 1957 Chevrolet, the Texas Highway Patrol, the U.S. Border Patrol, Customs officials at the border, and Mexican police were notified to arrest the trio. As a result, three very surprised men, one of whom owned a green Chevy, had their Mexican vacation rudely interrupted when they were arrested by Mexican police and hustled back to Houston. Having no gambling experience beyond church bingo games, they were released with apologies. Johnny, however, still smelled Norris and put out an all-points bulletin asking that the man be arrested on sight.

Checking all possible angles, Johnny learned that the night after the murder a green 1957 Chevrolet was spotted by a traffic patrol officer speeding down a Houston street. The officer gave chase but he lost the auto in traffic. He did, however, notice that the occupants threw several objects out the window of the car during the pursuit. Early the next morning Johnny and the traffic officer retraced the route of the chase and after a long search found two pistols laying in grass, luckily unnoticed by passers-by.

Johnny took the two weapons to the sheriff's office and had police again round up all the Damon Runyon types. One of the men admitted one of the pistols belonged to him. He said he had been held up at gunpoint by Gene Paul Norris and an accomplice who took "a lot of money and my pistol." From the serial numbers on the other pistol, it was traced to an underworld character named Cecil Green who, it was rumored, had been gunned down by Norris on a hit paid for by other gangsters. Shortly after Norris collected his fee, he married the widow Green.

A few days later, Klevenhagen received word from a young Temple, Texas police officer that an ex-convict named William Carl Humphrey, thirty-five, had been arrested the previous night for public drunkenness and was released the following morning after paying a fine. The officer remembered that Humphrey was wearing a large, gaudy gold ring in the form of a horseshoe and that the face of the horseshoe was sprinkled with small diamonds. Hearing about the Brannan murder, the policeman wondered if that was the kind of ring a rich horse bookie might wear. It was. Friends of Brannan recognized the description as the ring Brannan always wore "for luck." That cinched it for Klevenhagen, and the ranger filed murder charges against Norris and Humphrey. All that remained was to find them.

After Johnny turned Houston and Galveston upside down searching for the two killers, he received a telephone call from Fort Worth Police Chief Cato Hightower, who had a hot tip that Norris and Humphrey were in Fort Worth. Rumors in the underworld had it they were planning a big heist and perhaps, he said, Johnny might like to come up and take a look. The ranger let out a great whoop, packaged his arrest warrants, and took the next flight north.

When he reached Fort Worth, he met with Chief Hightower and Texas Ranger Captain Jay Banks. Banks was the tall, muscular ranger who modeled for the big bronze statue of a Texas Ranger that greets visitors in the lobby of the Dallas Love Field airport terminal. Together the three lawmen probed every stool pigeon, parolee, and ex-convict in the area. Finally a former convict working at a menial job at Carswell Air Force Base turned up in Hightower's office and revealed a bizarre plot.

Norris, he said, approached him and demanded he give him the name of an employee of the branch of the Fort Worth National Bank located at Carswell. When the man objected, saying he wanted no part of an illegal scheme, Norris threatened to kill his wife and children. Knowing Norris was not bluffing, the man gave him the name of a female employee of the bank who lived with her twelve-year-old son on Meandering Road in Fort Worth. Then, becoming frightened, the man went to the police to tell them of the plot.

Norris, he said, learned that the Carswell payroll was to be delivered to the base's branch bank on Tuesday morning, April 30. Norris and Humphrey planned to drive to the woman's house early Tuesday morning and either kill her and her son or take them hostage. They would seize her automobile, which had a windshield sticker granting admission to the base, and then use her door keys to open the bank's outer doors. When they reached the bank lobby, they would seize bank employees as they came to work and at gunpoint make them open the safe and cash drawers.

When the armored car guards entered the bank carrying more than $500,000 in cash, they would be held up, then tied up, and along with the rest of the bank employees would be locked in the bank's vault. With the half million in small and virtually untraceable bills and the rest of the bank's money, they would flee in the woman's automobile. After driving to the woman's house, they would dump her car and escape in their automobile. It was a wild and crazy scheme, but it just might have worked if the police had not been tipped off.

That evening Johnny and Jay Banks visited the woman and told her of the plot. She was visibly shocked, but after they assured her they would keep her house under surveillance and intercept Norris before he could get to her, she agreed to cooperate. She agreed she would tell no one about the plot and would do nothing out of her usual routine.

Taking no chances, Chief Hightower detailed teams of four crack shots to stake out the house twenty-four hours a day in case the bandits came early. On Monday, April 29 at 3:00 P.M., Johnny, Banks, and Hightower were driving near the woman's home when they spotted Norris and Humphrey in an automobile. They were probably making a trial run of the route they would take in preparation for Tuesday's strike.

Banks jammed his foot down on the accelerator and pulled up alongside the bandits and ordered them to pull over to the curb. Startled, Norris pulled out a revolver, Humphrey stepped on the gas, and they took off at high speed. There followed an hour-long running gun battle as Norris fired at the pursuing lawmen and they in turn leaned out the windows of their car and blasted away. Soon three more police cars joined the chase as it roared north-westward through quiet residential neighborhoods. Careening through the streets, they narrowly missed women who frantically wheeled baby carriages out of their way. They scattered lunch-bound schoolchildren who fled into front yards to escape from the screaming sirens, screeching tires, and booming gunshots. Undeterred by the women and children, Norris kept up a constant gunfire with pistol and shotgun at his pursuers. As the chase broke out into more open country, the bandit car turned onto State Highway 199 North and the speeds zoomed up to 120 miles per hour.

As Banks see-sawed his auto across the road and dodged Norris's shotgun blasts, Klevenhagen leaned out one window firing his .45 while Hightower blasted away from the back seat with a .38. After they sped five miles on the highway, the bandit car suddenly lurched off the blacktop and onto a winding, muddy dirt road near the little village of Springtown where the road twisted along the banks of Walnut Creek. Finally taking a turn too fast and skidding in the slick mud, Humphrey lost control and the auto careened off the roadway and smashed into two trees.

Shaken, Norris and Humphrey stumbled out of the wreckage, grabbed their guns, and started running through a wooded area near the creek as the lawmen's cars screeched into spinning stops on the slick road. Soon a dozen lawmen leaped from their cars and took up the pursuit on foot.

Norris turned, spotted Klevenhagen, smiled and snapped a shot in his direction, then started running across the creek. Humphrey, already in midstream, was staggered by a bullet from the posse but kept his balance and struggled through the flooded stream in water up to his waist as geysers of muddy water from police bullets splashed around him. He was hit again and again until he finally reached a small mud island in the middle of the creek. He stumbled on to it and fell dead with his body ripped by twenty-three bullets.

Norris, running upstream along the bank, was hit several times and was bleeding profusely, but he kept going. He intermittently turned and fired at Klevenhagen who kept coming straight at him. Finally, when he got within range, Johnny let go with his twelve-gauge shotgun. It proved to be the coup de grace. Norris spun around and fell face down into the mud, and his body slowly rolled into the creek. He was no longer smiling.

Later when newspapermen interviewed the bank teller, the attractive woman stated, "When they told me I was the intended kidnap victim, I was pretty scared. I knew I was being protected but still it was difficult to sleep at night, and I have recently noticed a few gray hairs." Her twelve-year-old son, however, lamented, "Mom didn't tell me about it. It would have been exciting. I missed all the fun."

A few days later, when Norris's mother and his twenty-four-year-old wife drove to Fort Worth to claim his body, they were driving a green 1957 Plymouth. After the distraught mother told newspapermen, "I don't understand it at all. Gene was such a good boy." Chief Hightower responded, "He was a madman." His was the more accurate description.

John Klevenhagen wrote one of his terse official reports to Austin Ranger headquarters, "Subjects resisted arrest and fired on Rangers. Subjects were killed."

CHAPTER 18

Alton's Demons

After the demons had come and gone, Alton would trek to the banks of Yegua Creek or one of the other tributaries of the Brazos River. Someone once told him the original name of the river given by the Spaniards was Brazos de Dios, the arms of God. He would find a sandy bank on the creek, take off all his clothes and arms outstretched, form his body into a cross and feel that he, Alton Golden Halson, lay in the arms of God.

On a summer day he would often find shade under the branches of the native yaupon shrubs. That too was symbolic, for the Indians claimed yaupon leaves were a purgative that could cleanse one from moral defilement and guilt.

That July 7, 1956, as he lay naked on the bank of the Yegua, the sun was hot and the little foxes, racoons, and rabbits were stilled in the heat. As he watched a leaf slowly meander down the creek, propelled by a drowsy current, he thought how it was too hot even for the water moccasins to swim. But it was restful to lie in the lush greenery after the violence of the nights and days when the demons had really gotten to him.

They came as always when he mixed his hell's brew of warm beer, cheap wine, and headache powders into a big jug and quickly drank it all down. He had done it before and it had always caused him much trouble. A year ago he was released from that hellish mental institution in California that his mother had cajoled him into entering and to which he swore he would never return.

He saved enough money to buy a bus ticket to Somerville, Texas, where he would live with his aging father. But Tilman Halson was not happy to see his son because he always created great troubles for the old man, so Alton was sent to live with his grandmother, Mrs. Lillie Deerman.

Somerville was a quiet village of not much more than a thousand people. A railroad town, it boasted a large creosote plant which processed railroad ties, and its only distinct feature was a modern motel of remodeled boxcars with a caboose used as a lunchroom. It was an agricultural area of hard-working, churchgoing, law-abiding people whose main income derived from the cattle and poultry business.

The law in Somerville was forty-seven-year-old Constable Milton "Romeo" Lewis, an amiable giant of a man, who at six-foot-four inches and more than two hundred pounds of country muscle towered over Alton whenever they met. The constable's older daughter, Janice, described him as a man "who loved people and was so tenderhearted that he couldn't stand seeing a child spanked. He tried to help Alton even though he often had to arrest him. He always reached out to people and often gave money to people down on their luck."

By contrast, Alton was a quiet, polite little man with a faint trace of mustache, who at thirty-six years of age was barely five feet tall and weighed in at a dainty one hundred and twenty pounds. Most people understood that he was not quite right in the head, which was why he didn't work but lived on a small pension. He could, however, be a nuisance because of his proclivity for taking off all his clothes and lying down in the nearest field to watch the clouds drifting by, blown by the lazy summer winds.

Earlier in the year, rancher Charlie Hardt, who owned land south of downtown Somerville, found Alton lying naked under the shade of a tree in his pasture and called Constable Lewis to arrest him. There were a few other instances of Alton's "strangeness," which could be tolerated, so the big lawman befriended the little man and gained rapport with him. But soon afterwards Alton started drinking his potent mixture of booze and medicine, and his actions turned from strange to violent.

Back in June, Alton had turned mean and Constable Lewis reported, "I had to arrest him after he beat up his grandmother." Alton was locked up for a few days and released when the grandmother refused to press charges. Lewis remarked later, "He never gave me any trouble, and he was just as polite as could be." On another occasion, Alton, while roaring drunk, wandered down the streets of Somerville in the wee hours of the morning shooting a .38-caliber revolver into the air. No one was hurt, but again Constable Lewis took him into custody, and he was later sent to a state mental hospital at Rusk, Texas. After a spell there, he was released into the custody of his put-upon grandmother.

Alton was quiet for a while, mostly dreaming in the sun along the banks of the creek, but on Thursday night, July 5, his demons possessed him again. In his fevered state Alton

A husky, friendly man, Constable Milton Lewis, shown with his wife Marguerite, was seriously wounded by the man he befriended.

mixed up his brew. He poured bottles of beer, cheap red wine, and packages of headache powders into a jug, stirred it up, and gulped it down. He took his revolver and went out into the neighborhood streets. Babbling and cursing at imaginary enemies, he stalked down the quiet streets shooting at random into the air and occasionally at a house.

Annoyed or just plain scared, residents rang Constable Lewis's telephone off the hook that night. Lewis dressed, got into his automobile, and drove to Alton's neighborhood, but when he got there all was quiet and the disturbed man was nowhere to be seen. Lewis also received a telephone call from Alton's father, Tilman Halson, who pleaded, "Constable, please arrest my son before he hurts someone or himself."

Early Friday morning, July 6, the constable started searching, driving up and down the creek areas where he expected to find him naked and lying in the sun, but Alton was not to be found. Later that morning Lewis drove back into town, and about 10:15 A.M. he saw him wandering down the street, shoeless, wearing only a pair of blue pants and a loose tan sport shirt. The constable drove up to him, braked, and called, "Alton, I want to talk to you." Alton, stopped, a vague look on his face, and walked over to the automobile.

"I know you are looking for me," Alton said, blank faced, "but this is what you are going to get." He reached inside his shirt, pulled out a .38-caliber revolver, and without another word started shooting. Three bullets struck the surprised constable in the stomach. In an effort to get away, Lewis fell out of the car and onto the street.

The daughter of Constable Lewis, sixteen-year-old Janice heard the shots and ran to her father who was lying in the street bleeding from three gunshot wounds.

Constable Lewis's daughter, Janice, a slender, pretty, sixteen-year-old, was in the backyard of the family home only a half block away, hanging up clothes on the wash line. "I heard what sounded like firecrackers going off," Janice said. "I thought it was the boy next door shooting them off, but something told me to investigate. I ran to the front yard, looked down the street and saw my daddy lying in the street. I ran toward him and Daddy yelled, 'Go back to the house, he will kill you,' but I still ran over to him anyway. I saw Alton standing there with a gun in his hand and I said, 'Get out of here. Get away from my dad.' He left and I stayed by Dad until help came."

191

A local man, Frank Connell, saw the shooting and ran to the constable's side. Lewis, blood gushing from three bullet holes, with a great effort drew his revolver and handed it to Connell, rasping, "Go get that fellow before he kills someone else," then he lapsed into semiconsciousness. Connell took the pistol and walked swiftly to the slowly departing Alton who was mumbling, "He won't bother me no more."

When Connell overtook him, Alton turned around and Connell said, "Throw down your gun and give up." Alton pulled out his .38 and a .45 automatic from his back pocket and said, "Let's start shooting." The two men, only a few feet away from each other and pointing guns at one another, seemed locked in what might be instant death for both. Suddenly two women ran into the street screaming, "Don't shoot, remember your wife and two children." Connell realized that not only the women but a small crowd gathering by the stricken constable would be in a direct line of fire if he and Alton engaged in a gunfight.

"I won't shoot," Connell said, lowering his pistol. Alton lowered his weapons, turned around, and walked away muttering.

Charlie Hardt, who had had Alton arrested a few months before, was working on a water tank in his pasture when he heard the shots. He saw Alton walking toward him with a gun in his hand. Hardt, exasperated, shouted, "Alton, what are you doing here shooting off a gun in my pasture? Now you get off my land, do you hear?" Alton looked at Hardt and meekly replied, "Okay, Captain" and wandered off. Hardt later must have considered that on that morning he was the luckiest man in Somerville.

A few minutes later Constable Cecil Sears spotted Alton near his father's house. As he approached the crazed man, Alton turned and fired a shot at him. Sears returned fire, and for a few moments the two blazed away at one another with no effect. After emptying his revolver Alton ran off into the brushy country at the edge of town, shouting he would shoot anyone who followed him. Sears, who had an artificial leg, could not follow him through the rough, tangled underbrush and reluctantly gave up the chase.

By this time a massive posse of lawmen from ten counties, civilian volunteers, state police, and Texas Rangers, numbering more than three hundred hard-eyed men were assembling in Somerville. Among them was the ubiquitous Johnny Klevenhagen.

On Friday morning two teenagers told police they saw Alton at the city dump heading toward Yegua Creek wearing only a tow sack and a belt. He carried a revolver and an automatic pistol in his hands. Soon light aircraft were flying low over the creek, and some lawmen were beating the bushes on foot while Johnny organized a mounted posse of thirty men. They combed the area in vain until the warden of Wynne State Prison Farm arrived on the scene with a yelping pack of eager bloodhounds.

Burleson County Sheriff Lewis Willard found the tan sport shirt Alton was wearing the morning of the shooting laying under a tall tree where it had apparently been thrown away. The sheriff figured Alton had climbed up to one of the higher branches to try and spot the posse's location, then moved on. The sheriff gave the shirt to a deputy, telling him to take it to where the bloodhounds were being assembled and give them a good sniff. Then he moved on down the creek, continuing the search.

As Sheriff Willard stalked on down the creek bank, he inadvertently provided the only light moment to what had become a grim probing into wild country where a crazed man with two pistols could easily ambush a pursuer. For when the bloodhounds got through sniffing the shirt, their handler, Dog Sergeant R.C. Kelton, gave them their heads.

With loud yelping and ears flapping, the pack raced off toward the creek bottoms, outdistancing the lawmen running behind them. After a lung-blowing chase the posse closed on the pack, which was leaping at the trunk of a tree with loud howls and baring of teeth. Up among the top branches the posse saw a figure clinging to a limb and expressing his opinion of the bloodhounds with some basic Anglo-Saxon expletives. The treed man was Sheriff Willard, who had apparently left his own scent on the shirt.

After the bloodhounds were put on another track, they soon found a pair of underwear shorts thrown onto a bush. The hunt continued most of the night, and after only a few hours' rest, early the next morning the chase began anew. Soon the hounds found Alton's blue trousers tossed on the marshy ground, and they knew they were getting close.

As Alton lay naked, warming himself in the late afternoon sun, he was listening to the call of a mockingbird and the gentle rustling of quail among the reeds lining the bank of the creek. But then he heard a faint discordant sound, and as it came nearer he identified it as the yelping of bloodhounds. He picked up the brown suede jacket he had stolen from a farmhouse and wrapped it around his waist, checked the .38 and the .45 to be sure they were loaded, and crawled behind the makeshift breastworks he had constructed from shrubs and dead limbs. Then he waited.

On Saturday July 7, Klevenhagen was searching the north side of Yegua Creek when he received word that the hounds had caught up with Alton. The ranger rode across the creek and cantered up to the site of Green Mountain, actually a large hill, along the creek a few miles south of Somerville. There he found the posse had boxed Alton into a small patch of chaparral and brush he was using as a fort.

Dismounting, he held a council of war with the posse members. "Watch out, Johnny," one of them cautioned,

"He's in cover in that brush and he's shooting at anybody that moves." Johnny grunted, walked back to the big bay horse, and swung back into the saddle. He slung his shotgun into a saddle scabbard, held the reins in one hand and his .45 automatic in the other, spurred the bay into a gallop, and rode up to within a few feet of the brush fort.

"This is Texas Ranger Johnny Klevenhagen speaking, Alton; come out with your hands up and you won't be harmed," he shouted.

Alton replied, "I surrender," and stepped out into the open with his hands stretched high in the air. But there was still a pistol in each hand and a wild look in his eyes.

Suddenly, he dropped his arms and started shooting at the ranger. The gunshots spooked Klevenhagen's horse and a bullet just missed his ear. There followed a crazed ballet as the horse reared and plunged. Johnny was trying to control the panicked animal with one hand on the reins while blasting back at Alton with his .45 in the other hand, and at the same time Alton was dancing around trying to get a clear shot at the ranger. More than a dozen shots were fired at a range of fifteen feet, and they all missed.

Johnny later related, "My horse jumped so badly when I fired, I decided to get off, grabbing my shotgun as I did so. I shouted again for Alton to surrender but he kept shooting so I let him have it with my shotgun twice."

One blast of double aught buckshot hit Alton dead center, and the second blew half his head away. Alton fell backward onto the soft ground, his arms outstretched; his demons would haunt him no more. Johnny remounted and rode back to the posse saying, "Cancel the request for more horses. Call for an ambulance and a coroner. Subject is dead." The seventy-eight-hour manhunt was over.

Later that day Janice and other members of the family visited at St. Jude's Hospital in Brenham where Constable

Lewis was recovering from surgery in which two bullets were removed from his stomach. Milton was delighted to see his daughter since before he passed out he had feared Alton had killed her.

The following day Klevenhagen visited the constable with a going away gift. Johnny presented Milton the .38 revolver that Alton had used to shoot him. Johnny told him, "I thought you might like as a souvenir the pistol that nearly took your life." He also told the constable, "Without those dogs from the prison farm I don't think we would have ever been able to track Alton down in that brush."

The big constable recovered quickly, although for the rest of his long life he carried the third of the .38 slugs buried in his belly. He later became a deputy sheriff for Burleson County and served in law enforcement work for many years. According to Burleson County Sheriff Gene Barber, "In addition to his law enforcement duties, Lewis operated the best darn restaurant in Somerville," and Janice recalled it was famous with the visiting railroad men for "our home baked pies."

She recalled, "In our City Café we had the town's fire bell, and whenever a fire broke out anywhere near Somerville, Daddy would ring the bell to summon the volunteer firefighters."

Ranger Klevenhagen sent in one of his now famous terse reports to Ranger headquarters in Austin, "Searched on foot, horseback, and in cars. After 75 hours, located subject in Yegua Creek bottom. Subject resisted and fired on Ranger Klevenhagen. Subject was killed."

But it was not quite that simple for the ranger. John Klevenhagen Jr. said, "My dad felt very bad about the shooting. He knew Alton was mentally deficient, but when the man kept shooting at him, he had no choice but to shoot him." As usual, however, Klevenhagen kept to his ideal. He always let the other fellow shoot first before he returned fire. Many of his friends said it was a miracle he wasn't killed in his many gunfights. John Jr. said that when Johnny found out Alton's family was destitute, he dug down into his own pocket and paid for a gravestone to be placed at the cemetery. "It was typical of Dad," John Jr. added.

CHAPTER 19

The Free State of Galveston

In 1817 pirate Jean Laffite sailed into Galveston Bay, landed on the beach, and founded a settlement called Maison Rouge. It didn't last long, but the pirate mentality remained for 150 years.

Galveston Island is twenty-seven miles long and less than three miles wide at its widest part. It consists of hard-packed sand only a few feet above sea level. Its history somewhat mirrors its climate and the surrounding sea.

Mostly it is tranquil, with soft sea breezes and small waves lapping the sandy shore under a warm sun and a cloudless pale blue sky. When hurricane winds blow in late summer and early autumn, however, it can become a hell of crashing walls of water that twist steel and concrete beams into tortured pretzels and wind that blows glass windows into flying shrapnel-like missiles and lifts and slings roofs into piles of tangled debris.

Galveston's history has followed similar patterns. By the mid-nineteenth century it had become a flourishing port, shipping cotton, sugar cane, and cattle to the east coast of the United States and to Europe. As such it had the usual outlets for sailor vices, prostitution and booze.

During the Civil War it was fought over twice. A Union invasion army seized the town in 1862, but resurgent Confederates recaptured it after a hard-fought battle in 1863. It functioned throughout the war as a haven for blockade runners who slipped by the Union fleet guarding the harbor.

Galveston's second biggest trade, tourism, began to flourish late in the century when excursion trains from the growing Houston metropolis brought carloads of straw-hatted and ribbon-bonneted folks to frolic in the warm waters, picnic on the beach, and enjoy the seafood caught fresh every day. Both the rough sailors and the more genteel tourists enjoyed the island without conflict.

The idyll ended in September 1900 when a hurricane hit the island with 120-mile-an-hour winds. A tidal wave smashed across the city and put downtown under five feet of water, demolished half the city's buildings, and killed more than 6,000 people. The survivors constructed a massive concrete seawall and rebuilt the city, which quickly flourished.

A new era was about to open when, in 1910, two Sicilian barbers named Rose and Sam Maceo moved to the island. They were minor smugglers until the advent of Prohibition in 1919, when the island became the darling of "rum-runners" whose fast speedboats loaded wine and hard liquors from hulking freighters hovering past the three-mile limit of the territorial waters of the United States. Then the swift powerboats, loaded with booze, zipped into the shallow inlets of the bay to unload for thirsty customers. They not only supplied the revived vice business in Galveston but serviced Houston and all points north.

In the competition for the bootlegging business, the Maceos conquered all their competitors either by force or guile and soon controlled all illegal liquor sales in the Galveston County area. Their operations were a monopoly, and it was rumored but never proved that competitors received a pair of concrete overshoes and were given the opportunity to walk on the bottom of the bay.

Quickly they expanded their business until they reigned over nightclubs, gambling, and prostitution. From the borders of the little mainland town of Dickinson, the Maceo-Dickinson Line was established. South of it vice flourished, and in the words of Cole Porter, "anything goes."

After national Prohibition was ended in 1933, Texas state law still forbade sales of liquor by the drink. In some "wet" counties one could buy a beer, but wine and hard alcohol could be sold only in licensed stores. When you dined in a restaurant and wanted wine or a highball, you purchased a bottle in a liquor store and took it with you; the restaurant would provide the mix. Any form of gambling and of course prostitution was against the law.

Galveston was different. Along Post Office Street, whorehouses boldly set red lights flashing at their doorways to attract customers, bars served mixed drinks openly, and dice tables, blackjack games, and slot machines filled many restaurants and bars. The Maceos loudly proclaimed "The Free State of Galveston."

The jewel of their operations was the Balinese Room, a restaurant built on a massive pier which extended more than two hundred feet beyond the seawall. Aside from the liquor violations in the restaurant and dance floor, there was a large T-head at the end of the pier where a variety of gambling tables catered to the high-rollers of the burgeoning oil and real estate empires being built in Houston.

Rose Maceo, the brains of the empire, was widely popular among most of the city's population. There was not a good cause, a charity bazaar, or a church fund-raiser in which he was not the main contributor.

Hollywood stars like Frank Sinatra, George Burns, Alice Faye, Jack Benny, and Jane Russell not only performed at the Balinese Room, they also volunteered their services to a variety of fund-raising activities for worthy causes.

The Maceos charitable contributions, however, paled beside their financial support of local and state politicians, and the family members were enthusiastic supporters of whoever was the reigning governor of Texas. On occasion there might be a momentary political falling out, a rare Galveston reform movement, or outcries from religious "drys" bringing pressure to enforce the law, and a few token raids were carried out.

On those occasions Texas Rangers would barge into gambling halls with sledgehammers and axes and for the benefit of news photographers, gleefully chop and bust up dice tables, roulette wheels, slot machines, and numerous liquor bottles. It might take a week for Galveston to return to business as usual.

Sometimes the raids were a farce. The Maceos were tipped off by Galvez County Sheriff Frank Biaggne, a hulking, genial fellow who was a regular recipient of Maceo largesse. He performed a Galveston version of Paul Revere, shouting, "The Rangers are coming. The Rangers are coming." Biaggne was not without charm, and he had a Yogi Berra sense of humor. Once when asked why he did not raid the Balinese Room and put an end to their illegal activities, he exclaimed, "They won't let me in. I'm not a member of the club."

In the Balinese Room or other targets, when the alarm was given, slot machines were folded into walls, roulette wheels were hidden, blackjack became genial bridge games, and cokes and beer replaced martinis and Scotch and water.

As the rangers moved through the labyrinthine hallway of the Balinese Room and entered into the big T-head, the band would strike up "The Eyes of Texas" and the master of ceremonies would implore, "Ladies and gentlemen, let's give a big round of applause for our very own Texas Rangers." There followed deafening applause. Most Texans loved it. The Texas Rangers were not amused.

The rangers were harnessed by political factions in Austin and could not make a move against Galveston unless they had specific orders from the governor or the state attorney general. It was to them a great source of frustration.

But the fun and games were coming to an end. Industrial growth in the Houston/Galveston area dimmed the previous economic reliance on the vice and tourist business, and reform movements began to blossom. In 1951 Sam Maceo died of cancer, and in 1953 Rose ascended to that big slot machine in the sky. Family members carried on amidst increasing reform pressure.

In 1956 the reformers flourished when crime-busting Will Wilson became attorney general of Texas. With the approval of Governor Allan Shivers and later incoming Governor Price Daniel, state and private investigators used undercover operations to procure evidence on all phases of Galveston vice.

In June 1957 a task force of law officers headed by Ranger Captain John Klevenhagen was ready to strike.

On June 11 Attorney General Wilson filed civil actions against forty-seven saloons, whorehouses, and gambling joints that covered the length and breath of the Maceo-Dickinson line. Injunctions were accepted by judges who filed restraining orders to close down illegal activities in

Galveston, Dickinson, Kemah, Texas City, and Algoa. The actions came as a result of undercover investigators who reported illegal dice games, roulette, blackjack, bingo, and slot machines in use as well as numerous liquor violations.

They also reported being solicited by women in six brothels. When they spurned the women's importunities, the prostitutes, they complained, became very abusive and used indecent language toward them.

Three nights later Johnny, accompanied by Ranger Ed Gooding and local police, led a posse that raided two night-clubs that ignored the restraining orders. Wielding a ten-pound sledgehammer, Johnny told newspaper report-ers, "This is the key that fits all slot machines and opens all doors."

On the evening of June 14 he smashed down the door of the L&M Club and reduced to splinters and junk metal a slot machine, dice table, and blackjack table. Leaving that wreckage, he moved to a late-night rendezvous for gam-blers named "Peaches' Place." There, using his "key," he entered through the shattered front door and proceeded to dismember additional slot machines and card tables.

The following night almost all gambling and illegal liquor sales stopped throughout Maceo land when unknown persons in local law enforcement tipped off oper-ators that Johnny would be on the loose with a posse of sixty sledgehammer and axe wielders. But for the gambling fraternity, the worst was yet to come.

On a tip from an informer, early on the morning of June 15, Johnny, Ranger Gooding, and a bevy of investigators from the attorney general's office boarded the Point Bolivar ferryboat, which crosses Galveston Bay from the city to the Bolivar Peninsula. The peninsula was a haven for fishermen whose small shacks stood just above the waterline.

Dominating the area is Fort Travis, built in 1896 to protect Galveston port from enemy navies. The fort, spread over many acres, is a series of massive concrete and steel gun emplacements for giant twelve-inch artillery pieces. There are concrete watchtowers for spotting enemy targets, massive earthen redoubts, and deep subterranean tunnels where the big gun ammunition was stored.

The army abandoned the fort at the conclusion of World War II, and some of the land was sold to private parties while the rest remains a public park.

Johnny's informant told him that when the first injunctions were filed restricting gambling, the more judicious operators had under cover of night spirited their expensive slot machines, marble tables, and roulette wheels into several large boats. They unloaded them at Fort Travis and hid them in one of the deep underground ammunition tunnels.

Once inside the fort, the posse made for a communications tunnel, and with flashlights glowing marched down the dank passageway until they came to a giant bunker once used to store twelve-inch shells and gunpowder. After Johnny's sledgehammer smashed down the bunker door, it was not dissimilar to entering a tomb of the ancient pharaohs.

When the place was lighted up, the metallic glint of scores of slots and pinball machines sparkled in the gloomy cave-like room. There was a treasure trove of roulette wheels stacked against the sides of the bunker, and bags of chips and boxes of playing cards lying on poker and blackjack tables.

After the posse had worked up a pleasant sweat demolishing the machines, Johnny led them to an abandoned and boarded-up army barracks. After smashing in the door, they found still more gambling paraphernalia, which was soon reduced to junk. An abandoned warehouse was next with

Ranger Captain Klevenhagen swings his sledgehammer to break up
a slot machine seized during the 1957 raids in Galveston.

the same destructive results. Then an arm-weary but
delighted posse bid farewell to the old coast artillery fort
and boarded the ferry back to Galveston.

Johnny reported that 350 slot machines, 150 pinball,
horse race, and bangtail machines as well as numerous roulette wheels and card tables were turned into rubbish by the
ranger posse. The monetary damage was estimated at more
than $350,000, not an insignificant sum in 1957 dollars.
And since a new federal law prohibited transporting gambling machines across state lines, it was more than a
financial loss since the machines could never be replaced.

In one of his rare statements to the press, Johnny
remarked, "The raid hit the jackpot for the state of Texas."

There were still a few reckless gamblers who somehow did not get the message that the old days were over. They soon learned better.

The June 18 front page of the *Houston Post* reported, "A wrecking crew headed by Texas Ranger Captain John Klevenhagen marched up and down Galveston for hours Monday night smashing in doors and gambling devices with sledgehammers."

Accompanied by Gooding and Oliver, a member of the attorney general's staff, and two Galveston policemen, Johnny made a destructive visitation to more than a dozen bars and gambling dens. He also located twenty-four slot machines stashed in a garage. The night's raids ended at the Rio Grande Tavern and Club after Johnny bashed in the door, and the posse became arm weary after demolishing twenty-five slots, two pool tables, and a roulette wheel. "Besides," Johnny complained, "I drafted a newspaper reporter to do some machine bashing, and after a few licks he broke the handle of my sledgehammer." It was not a bad night's work.

During the course of one swoop, Johnny seized two submachine guns. One was a Model 55 Reising .45-caliber with folding stock, a type used by the U.S. Marine Corps during World War II. The other was a 9mm Beretta. Both weapons were put to use by the Texas Rangers for a number of years before they were donated to the Texas Ranger Museum located at Ft. Fisher in Waco, Texas.

If Johnny's raids broke the back of Galveston's vice empire, the final nail in the coffin was a statement by Governor Price Daniel who vowed, "If local officials will not enforce the law in Galveston, Texas Rangers will be moved in and kept there until unlawful actions are ended." It was the end of an era for the rambunctious old island.

Johnny later told his son, John Jr., "I made many dice handlers, blackjack dealers, roulette wheel croupiers, and assorted gamblers wealthy men. Driven out of Galveston, they moved to Las Vegas and became rich."

"Galveston," he said later, "is the only area in Texas that compares to Duval County. It's so controlled that you cannot trust anyone. Some of the people there would sell out anyone or anything for a dollar."

After the Galveston cleanup, the ranger captain said, "When it comes to gambling and liquor sales, people and legislators need to understand that the law cannot enforce morals. If the majority of the people decide they want gambling and mixed drinks, let them have it. But let the state of Texas enforce regulations to keep it under control."

Today, Texas allows mixed drinks and there is a controlled state lottery. It took several decades, but finally the legislature came around to Johnny's way of thinking.

CHAPTER 20

Trail's End

By 1957 murder, a by-product of Houston's massive growth and blossoming wealth, had become a Frankenstein monster. The famed evangelist Billy Graham awarded the city the dubious title of "Murder Capital of the United States." In 1957 the city, with a population of 900,000, had racked up 137 murders, which on a per capita basis was the highest in the country.

Seventy percent were committed by African-Americans, and the rest were, in the cynical words of a female news reporter, "Just misdemeanor white-trash murders." More perplexing to folks other than Texans were the trivial causes of many of the killings and the very light penalties passed out by the courts to those few convicted. A potpourri of slayings: One man shot a waiter to death because he did not put enough beans in his bowl of chili. A woman shot and killed her father with the sole explanation, "I did it just for the hell of it." One man was killed in a bar because he refused to loan another man a nickel for a telephone call. A wife, angered because her husband laughingly sprayed her with a garden hose, shot and killed him.

Another wife blasted her spouse into eternity with a shotgun because he had spit out some black-eyed peas she had cooked for him. Many of the killings occurred in beer joints when boozed-up patrons got into arguments over the relative merits of football teams and in the "Code of the West" shot out their differences.

A throwback to "Southern Honor" was the virtual immunity from prosecution when one spouse killed the other for infidelity or for what was colloquially known as "slipping around." One enraged husband shot a man to death because he saw his wife sitting in an automobile with him. The killer defended his action on the grounds that "They were setting a bad example."

One year the infamous Percy Foreman defended thirteen women who killed their husbands. Twelve got off scot free and the other received only a five-year suspended sentence. As *Time Magazine* reported, "Of the 137 killings in 1957, only twenty-seven cases went to trial. One defendant received the death penalty, one got life imprisonment, and the rest received only a few years in jail or suspended sentences."

Theft, however, was treated more seriously. The author remembers a case where a man, after an argument, shot his estranged wife five times, killing her. Then panicking and trying to escape, he ran out into the street and stole a nearby automobile. He was quickly caught and brought to trial. Taking the stand in his defense, he accused the deceased wife of "slipping around." The jury returned a verdict of guilty on both counts of murder and automobile theft. He was awarded a five-year suspended sentence for the murder of his wife but was sent to the state prison for five to ten years for theft of the automobile. As he was being led away to jail he kept murmuring, "Why the hell did I have to go and steal that car?"

With all this carnage, Klevenhagen wasn't sure how many murder cases he solved, but a minimum estimate over a three-year period was around 125. And working through many nights, living on coffee, cigarettes, and adrenaline, were taking a toll on the ranger's health.

In September 1957 Klevenhagen was promoted to Texas Ranger captain, a position that many lawmen considered the pinnacle of a career in law enforcement. The promotion entitled him to a salary of $390 per month. The increased responsibilities, however, only heaped more burdens on an already tiring man. Even though Johnny was described by one lawman as "A man so tough and so cool in danger that he could sit on a red-hot stove and spit ice water," the strain of chronic overwork was catching up to him.

By the time he traded in his ranger badge, the five-pointed star supported by a wheel forged from a Mexican silver peso, for his captain's badge fashioned from a Mexican fifty-peso gold piece, he had become gaunt and hollow eyed, his face streaked with lines of fatigue.

Most of his limited spare time he spent with John Jr. and his wife, Viola. For the even rarer leisure time he saved for himself, he went fishing on the boat or hunting on the ranch of his closest friend, James Marion "Silver Dollar Jim" West.

"Silver Dollar Jim" was the paradigm of the flamboyant, high-living, Houston oil millionaire. He was famous for carrying pocketfuls of silver dollars with which he generously tipped everyone who performed the slightest service. Sometimes, when he saw a bunch of children playing, he would stop his automobile and toss handfuls of silver dollars and watch the kids happily scramble for them while his hearty laugh blended in with their squeals of delight.

At a later date it was determined that a horde of silver dollars weighing more than eight tons was stacked in an

During a rare vacation, Johnny with two friends shows the results of the hunt on "Silver Dollar Jim" West's ranch.

underground room in his River Oaks mansion. It amounted to more than $300,000.

He owned a fleet of forty-one lengthy Cadillacs, all of them painted in his favorite shade of blue and spouting a massive forest of aerials tuned to police frequencies. For West was what was called a "police buff," that breed of wannabees that ride with police patrolmen and experience vicariously the dangers, the adrenaline rush, and the infinite variety of police work.

Unlike most buffs, Jim West was a welcome help rather than a nuisance. His expensive shortwave radio equipment could pick up signals that would otherwise be lost or garbled to ordinary police patrol cars in the concrete canyons of Houston. Worn out officers after a long night's vigil perked up when Jim arrived at the scene of a ferocious auto accident, a flaming building, or a sweaty search through a swampy Houston bayou, bringing hot coffee, sandwiches, or other treats.

As a young police reporter, the author recalls being routed out of bed at midnight by a city editor whose instructions were to get up and cover a search for a missing ten-year-old girl. It was a hot, sultry night in August when the humidity and the moisture in the air turned a starched shirt into a damp rag in minutes. After hours of searching the brush and bayou banks near the girl's home, police, reporters, frantic parents, and volunteering neighbors let out a rousing cheer when "Silver Dollar Jim" pulled up in his blue limousine convertible and, with his usual flair and wide smile, began dispensing trays of ice cream to the hot, tired, and sweaty searchers. (After hours of beating the brush, it turned out that the girl forgot to tell her parents she was spending the night at a pajama party with a friend.)

Jim West was a man who loved and respected policemen, and they in turn reciprocated his camaraderie.

Recognizing his genuine help to police officers, he was awarded an honorary Special Texas Ranger's Commission that authorized him to wear a badge and carry a gun, and his automobile radios were an integral part of the police communications network.

West's arrival on a crime scene was an event unto itself. He often came dressed in an old flannel shirt whose collar points were made of platinum, blue jeans, a twenty-gallon cowboy hat perched on his head, a gold-handled .45-caliber six-gun tucked into a jeweled holster strapped to his side, a Special Texas Ranger badge embedded with nine glittering diamonds pinned to his shirt, and waving an almost foot-long cigar.

But West had a genuine concern for the welfare of police officers. When budgets were tight with both the city of Houston and Harris County governments, he spent a considerable sum of his own money to buy law enforcement officers life-saving bulletproof vests.

And when he learned through the grapevine that an officer or a member of his family needed medical attention they could not afford, it was Jim West who procured for them the finest doctors and the most accomplished surgeons. He picked up the bills, considering it a service to the men who selflessly guarded the public.

Knowing that police officers were horribly underpaid for the hours they worked and the risks they took, when an officer he knew was planning a vacation, West would drive one of his big blue Cadillacs to the officer's house, hand him the keys to the car and a credit card, saying, "You and your family have a good time."

For all that, the deep abiding friendship between West and Klevenhagen was a bonding of opposites. Johnny was tall and lean, his trim khaki pants and coat immaculately pressed, often grim-visaged, somewhat remote and sparing of words. "Silver Dollar Jim," on the other hand, was short, paunchy, flamboyantly attired, smiling, warm, and loquacious. Perhaps the attraction between the two was that under John's ranger mask of cool efficiency and dedication to duty was the same almost tender, warm concern for people that West showed outwardly.

Texas Ranger Edgar D. Gooding, who was assigned to Klevenhagen's company in June 1957, said, "The two men were like brothers." In early December 1957 "Silver Dollar Jim" was severely stricken with a deadly attack of his chronic diabetes. During that period, Viola said, her husband "was working too hard, never rested, and would come home exhausted."

An additional strain was added when Johnny came off duty, according to Ranger Gooding. "He would go to the hospital and stay up all night by his friend's bedside. I don't know if he ever slept," Gooding said. "He would come to work the next morning with black circles under his eyes and deeper lines in his face."

On December 18, after lingering for days, "Silver Dollar Jim" West died. He was only fifty-five years old. At three o'clock in the afternoon of December 20, Johnny was a pallbearer at his friend's funeral. Returning from the services late that afternoon, Johnny was stricken with a heart attack and rushed to a hospital.

After too short a time recuperating in the hospital, restless, Johnny went back to work. It was against the advice of his doctors who advised him to retire and take life easy. After all, they said, he had been a police officer for twenty-seven years, of which seventeen years had been spent in the Rangers, and the physical and mental strain in addition to the loss of three-fourths of his stomach to ulcers in 1946 would have drained the physical resources of half a dozen men. But John was adamant.

Johnny and his wife, Viola, posed for this photograph
shortly after his recovery from his first heart attack.

He told a *New York News* reporter, "I wouldn't want to be anything else but a Ranger. I aimed to be one when I was a kid. It's more of a way of life than it is a job, and it's an honor to wear the badge.

"A man doesn't just join this outfit, you know. He's picked out—really hand picked, too. There isn't a peace officer in Texas who wouldn't give his eyeteeth to get on the force."

Ranger Ed Gooding said that after Johnny returned to duty, he offered to do all the driving when the two of them went out on a case, but "Johnny looked at me with those steely blue eyes and said, 'No I'll drive. I might wear out but I won't rust out.' Johnny was a let's go guy, and there was a fire of duty burning in him that even a heart attack couldn't burn out.

"He would work all night, go home, bathe, shave, put on clean clothes, and go back on a case. Ranger Ed Oliver and I on a weekend would say, 'let's go fishing on Chocolate Bayou,' but he would beg off, and while Ed and I were fishing on the bayou over a weekend, Johnny would be working."

On April 21, 1958, Homer Garrison, the Director of the Texas Department of Public Safety who had appointed Johnny as a Ranger, wrote to him:

> I have just finished reading your report for the week ending March 29th and find that you put in a total of 79 hours for that *week*. You know that I appreciate your effort to "get the job done" but that is just too many hours for you to be working under your present physical condition. You have contributed so much to the Department of Public Safety that I do not intend to let you, at this late date, endanger your health. Seriously, Johnny, I am giving you an order now that you must comply with your doctor's orders

and cut down your number of hours. It is going to be difficult, of course, because you are energetic and conscientious but, on the other hand, you must do this.

With very best personal regards, I am sincerely your friend.

Homer Garrison, Director.

It was a futile effort. As the Reverend Roy Mayfield of Conroe Baptist Church later eulogized, "John Klevenhagen was a man so dedicated that his body literally burned itself out in service to his fellow man."

Ironically, it happened not while in pursuit of a dangerous criminal but during a rare time when Johnny took time off on Saturday, November 15, 1958. He was attending the Rice University-Texas A&M football game at Rice Stadium in Houston with Buster Kern. His son, John Jr., a student at Texas A&M was watching the game with friends in the student section of the stadium.

During the game Johnny felt a sudden pain, excused himself, and went down to the corridor behind the stands for water to take a heart pill his doctors had prescribed. Suddenly he staggered and collapsed. Terrified bystanders called for the ambulance that is always in attendance at Texas football games. He was immediately rushed to the hospital, given emergency treatment, and put under an oxygen tent.

Viola rushed to his side, and later other members of the family joined her at Houston's Methodist Hospital. Physicians there issued a statement on Monday that Johnny was "handling the attack well" but admitted that his heart was still too weak from his previous attack to perform an operation.

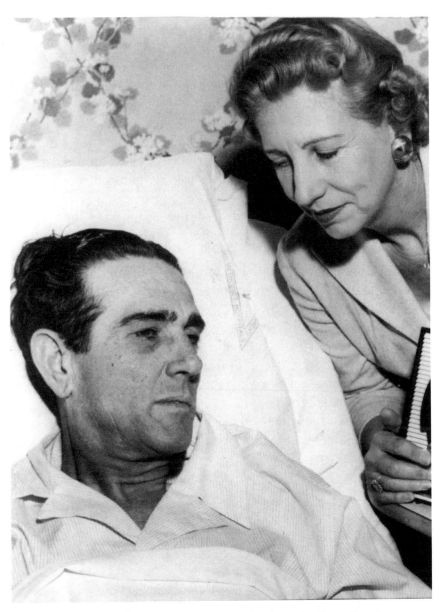

Viola watched by Johnny's bedside for days after he suffered
his second and fatal heart attack.
(Photo courtesy of Houston Public Library)

Viola stayed by his side for twelve agonizing days and nights sleeping on a cot beside his bed. At 3:30 A.M. on November 26, Johnny wakened from sleep feeling some pain. Viola said, "He knew he was going. He kept telling me good-bye." Then he died. And a legend was born.

Viola said, "He was a kind, dedicated man who just worked himself to death." He was only forty-six years old.

Shocked condolences from public officials, law enforcement officers, and his many friends poured into the Klevenhagen home. Many cards of regret came from men who had been arrested by Johnny. Plaintively, one ex-convict wrote, "Johnny was a good man. John is on one side of the fence and I am on the other. . . . I wish life could have been different and I was on John's side for he would be a good man to ride the river with.

"I've never had any love in my heart for a lawman, but I had only a brotherly feeling for Johnny as a real man and a real true blue friend. . . . I lost one of the best friends I ever had. . . . From a sad friend of the Tall Texan."

Texas Governor Price Daniel wrote, "The Texas Rangers have produced many great men in our state, and John Klevenhagen was one of the best. His death is a tragic loss to law enforcement in Texas."

Both houses of the Texas legislature passed a resolution recognizing "the great contribution to the state of Texas of Captain Klevenhagen" and adjourned in his honor.

Robert Gladney, former sheriff of Brazoria County, in a terse statement said, "He was a man short on words but heavy on effort."

Colonel Homer Garrison wrote:

"Captain Klevenhagen was one of the best officers Texas ever had. He combined the qualities of the frontier Ranger and his modern day counterpart. The lean leathery lawman was a peerless horseman and deadly, shot but he was also

The Klevenhagen gravesite in San Antonio.
Hundreds of peace officers from all over Texas
attended the funeral.

versed in ballistics, fingerprints, and other facets of advanced criminology. He was a licensed pilot and frequently used a plane in his duties. Such a combination made him a legend of law enforcement in the Southwest and his ability won him command of Texas Ranger Company A."

A more personal tribute, which tells much about Johnny's character, came from Ranger Jerome Preiss who joined the force in 1955. He told newsmen, "From the time I was ten years old and read about how Johnny solved so many cases, he became my role model and I determined that I too wanted to be a Texas Ranger just like him.

"What really inspired me about Johnny, when I got to know him personally, was that no matter how tired he was, how long he had worked, he always had time to pat some kid on the head who wanted to talk to him. That made him a great man in my eyes."

In a way, perhaps the most telling comment of all came from a grizzled old police officer who growled, "His name was an oath to the underworld."

A few days after his death, a twenty-automobile escort of police officers, sheriff's deputies, and Texas Rangers led by Buster Kern escorted Johnny's hearse on the 200-mile drive to the Alamo Funeral Home in San Antonio, where funeral services were held. Other automobiles carrying mourning officers came in from all over the state.

Among family and friends at the services were scores of hard-faced men packing badges and pistols. And there were not a few who had put their lives on the line with Johnny and who unashamedly wiped a tear-filled eye as they said good-bye.

CHAPTER 21

L'envoi

In later years, reminiscing about his father, John Jr. said, "Dad loved police work. It was his whole life. He often told me that if only he had an education he could have accomplished much more. He had to quit school at the eighth grade to help his parents on the ranch.

"Dad wanted me to take typing in school because he said, 'I can only use two fingers to type a report. You must be able to do better. I can make an arrest, but for lack of a proper education I can't make a speech.'

"He always told me, 'Whatever you do, you must strive to be the best there is. If you become a police officer, I want you to be the best there is.'"

John Jr. more than lived up to his father's wishes. When he reached his twenty-first birthday, he was hired as a deputy sheriff by his dad's old friend Buster Kern, and he soon proved he matched his father's cool courage and professional skill in dangerous situations.

On the cool evening of November 18, 1962, he stood in the middle of U.S. Highway 75 near Spring, Texas, to block the path of a desperate fugitive in a stolen car. The man,

Deputy Sheriff John J. Klevenhagen Jr. carried on the family tradition of dogged law enforcement, stopping a fleeing felon who tried to run him over with his automobile.

wanted by the FBI on a number of charges, had outdistanced two pursuing highway patrolmen in a running gunfight at more than 100 miles per hour. The only obstacle to his escape was Deputy John J. Klevenhagen Jr., who alerted by a radio message, cradled an automatic rifle in his arms and stood waiting in the road for the arrival of the fugitive's auto.

Soon the young officer spotted the car coming over a rise in the highway. As it approached, he waved his arm, signaling the fugitive to stop. Instead, as the auto's headlights illuminated the officer, the driver accelerated and aimed the vehicle straight at him.

Leaping to the side of the road, John Jr. squeezed the trigger of his rifle and sent a burst of fire into the automobile, smashing its engine block, blowing out three tires, and causing the car to come to a shuddering halt a few yards down the highway. The deputy ran up and slapped handcuffs on a shaking and docile criminal. After several pursuing police cars arrived on the scene, one veteran officer looked at the still shaking prisoner and then at the tall young deputy. "Like father, like son," he said.

During ensuing years John Jr. worked his way up the ladder of promotion by brains and dedication. At various times Klevenhagen rose to head the detective, law enforcement, and detention bureaus of the department. Following his father's advice, he put education high on his list of accomplishments, earning a bachelor's degree in police administration from the University of Houston, followed by a master's degree from Sam Houston State University. During a distinguished career in law enforcement, he graduated from the Federal Bureau of Investigation National Academy and became one of the few police officers selected to membership in the National Executive Institute of the FBI.

After twenty years' service, Klevenhagen resigned from the sheriff's department to enter the oil business. In 1984 he entered politics and was elected sheriff of Harris County, taking office in 1985. In 1988 and 1992 he was re-elected to that office by large margins. After serving a decade as sheriff, he re-entered private business by becoming a co-owner of an automobile dealership.

A lawman for thirty-seven years, when John Jr. joined the Harris County Sheriff's Department in 1961 it had 185 employees. By 1995 when he left office, it had swelled to more than 5,000. Houston's burgeoning population growth was matched by the growth of crime, and in 1985 when he was elected, there were 4,000 inmates in the county jail. When he left, the prison population had climbed to more than 12,000.

Civic minded, he worked diligently for dozens of community and youth groups, and his list of awards and certificates of appreciation would fill a dozen walls. He also

Harris County Sheriff John J. Klevenhagen Jr. celebrates his re-election during a Houston rodeo parade in 1992.

managed to teach courses at local colleges and the FBI Academy.

Tragically, he too was to die young. Suffering from an inoperable brain tumor, after a long illness he died May 13, 1999. He was only fifty-eight years old. He left behind his wife, Carolyn, son, John Klevenhagen III, daughter, Kara, and mother, Viola. More than 2,000 friends and law enforcement officers attended the funeral.

The *Houston Post* in an editorial wrote, "He was an honest lawman with an engaging smile and a firm handshake. He gave unlimited time and energy and service to numerous civic organizations. He served citizens of Harris County well....He was an excellent sheriff. But in addition to law enforcement, many will remember him as a good man who was always willing to support a good cause."

John and John Jr. left a record in Texas law enforcement that will be hard to equal and impossible to surpass. And they did it not only with dedication to duty but with kindness and understanding and a deep devotion to the people of Texas.

Bibliography

FOREWORD

Texas Ranger Captain Bill McDonald's quote is in Walter Prescott Webb, *The Texas Rangers*. University of Texas Press. Austin. 1965. Page 460.

CHAPTER 1

INTERVIEWS

John J. Klevenhagen Jr. November 24, 1998.

Carolyn Klevenhagen. November 24, 1998.

Viola Klevenhagen. November 24, 1998. Viola remembered that every Christmas, she and John Sr. would get dozens of cards from criminals Johnny had arrested, expressing good will and even affection. Many of the cards were mailed from Huntsville State Penitentiary.

MAGAZINES

True Detective Magazine. "Top Gun of the Texas Rangers" by Stan Redding. February 1963.

NEWSPAPERS

Houston Chronicle. April 14, 1958.
New York Sunday News. May 14, 1953.
San Antonio Light. July 20, 1940. November 28, 1958.

CHAPTER 2

BOOKS

Cude, Elton. *The Free and Wild Dukedom of Bexar*. Munguia Printers. San Antonio. 1958. Pages 286-288.

MAGAZINES

Official Detective Stories. "They'll Never Take Me Alive" by Duke
  Carver. January 15, 1938.
True Detective Mysteries. "Man Trap" by Owen Kilday, Chief of
  Police, San Antonio, Texas. February 1938.

CHAPTER 3

MAGAZINES

Confidential Detective Magazine. "Trail of the Red Eagle Tattoo" by
  David Montrose. March 23, 1938.

NEWSPAPERS

San Antonio Express. March 6, 13-17, 1938.

CHAPTER 4

BOOKS

Cude. *Dukedom of Bexar.*

MAGAZINES

Actual Detective Stories. "Where Are the Women From Alligator
  Joe's" by John R. Gray. December 1938 and January 1939.

NEWSPAPERS

San Antonio Light. October 14, 1938.

CHAPTER 5

INTERVIEWS

John J. Klevenhagen Jr. November 24, 1998.
Viola Klevenhagen. November 24, 1998.
Edgar D. Gooding, Texas Ranger, retired. December 17, 1998.

BOOKS

Charlton, Thomas Lee. *The Texas Department of Public Safety,
  1935-1957.* Thesis for the Graduate School of Government.
  University of Texas at Austin. 1961.
Proctor, Ben. *Just One Riot.* Eakin Press. Austin. 1991.

NEWSPAPERS

Houston Chronicle. April 14, 1958. November 7, 1971 (an interview with Texas Ranger Captain Edward Oliver).

New York Sunday News. May 17, 1953.

San Antonio Light. Undated clipping circa November 1958, in Klevenhagen biography files, Ft. Fisher, Texas Ranger Museum, Waco, Texas.

CHAPTER 6

BOOKS

Charlton. *The Texas Department of Public Safety.*

NEWSPAPERS

Houston Chronicle. September 24, 1967 (an interview with Texas Ranger Eddie Oliver and Harris County Chief Deputy Sheriff Lloyd Frazier). November 7, 1971.

Houston Post. June 16-19, 1943.

CHAPTER 7

INTERVIEWS

John J. Klevenhagen Sr. Circa 1950.
John J. Klevenhagen Jr. November 24, 1998.

NEWSPAPERS

Houston Chronicle. Undated clip. Klevenhagen files, Ft. Fisher.
Houston Post. August 25, 1945.

CHAPTER 8

INTERVIEWS

John J. Klevenhagen Sr. Circa 1950.
John J. Klevenhagen Jr. November 24, 1998.

MAGAZINES

True Detective Magazine. "Top Gun of the Texas Rangers" by Stan Redding. February 1963.

Chapters 9 and 10

Interviews

Author's recollections. Circa 1946-1952.
Edgar Gooding. February 1999.

Books

Dorman, Michael. *King of the Courtroom: Percy Foreman for the Defense.* Delacorte Press. New York. 1969.

Magazines

Life Magazine. March 28, 1949.

Newspapers

Houston Post. July 16-20, 30-31, 1949. October 17-20, 1949. March 1-4, 1952. August 24, 1969. August 16, 1970. April 9, 1981.
San Angelo Standard-Times. February 15-28, March 1-2, 1952.

Chapter 11

Books

Fuermann, George. *Land of the Big Rich,* Doubleday. Garden City, New York. 1951.

Magazines

Fortune Magazine. May 1949.
Life Magazine. March 28, 1949.
Newsweek Magazine. March 28, 1949.
Startling Detective Magazine. May 1950.

Newspapers

Galveston Daily News. April 5-8, 10-11, 13. May 4. November 27-30. December 16-17, 30-31, 1949.
Houston Post. April 5-6. November 27-28, 1949.

Chapter 12

Interviews

John J. Klevenhagen Sr. Circa 1950.
John J. Klevenhagen Jr. November 24, 1998.

Edgar Gooding. December 17, 1998.
John J. Klevenhagen III. August 28, 1999.
Viola Klevenhagen. August 28, 1999.
Carolyn Klevenhagen. August 28, 1999.

CHAPTER 13
INTERVIEWS

John J. Klevenhagen. Circa 1950.
John J. Klevenhagen Jr. November 24, 1998.

NEWSPAPERS

Houston Post. April 17-18, 1950. June 10-13, 1950. May 23, 1951.

CHAPTER 14
Author's recollections. Circa 1951-1953.

NEWSPAPERS

Houston Post. March 9-16, 1951.
San Antonio Express. July 2, 1950. March 9-16. April 4-5, 8. June 31, 1951. December 9, 1952. January 9-11, 1953.
San Antonio Light. November 1958.

CHAPTER 15
Author's recollections. Circa 1949-1954.

INTERVIEWS

Edgar Gooding. December 17, 1998.
Member of Freedom Party who did not wish his name revealed. December 1998.

BOOKS

Clark, John E. *The Fall of the Duke of Duval: A Prosecutor's Journal.* Eakin Press. Austin. 1995.
Nevin, David. *The Texans.* William Morrow & Co. New York. 1968.

NEWSPAPERS

Dallas Morning News. May 29, 1979.
Houston Post. July 30-31, 1949.

New York Times. February 5, 1954.
San Antonio Express. January 19-20, 1954.

CHAPTER 16
NEWSPAPERS

Houston Post. November 28-30, December 1-2, 1954. April 4, 1957.

CHAPTER 17
MAGAZINES

Texas Lawman. January 1946.
True Detective. "Top Gun of the Texas Rangers" by Stan Redding.

NEWSPAPERS

Dallas Morning News. March 16, 1942. May 29, 1979.
Fort Worth Star-Telegram. April 30, May 1, 1957.
Houston Chronicle Sunday Magazine. February 9, 1969.
Houston Post. March 17, 1942. April 17-20, 30. May 1, 1957.

CHAPTER 18
INTERVIEWS

Sheriff Gene Barber, Burleson County. April 29, 1999.
John J. Klevenhagen Jr. November 24, 1998.
Janice Rogers (nèe Lewis). April 24, 1999.
Paulett Srubar, Somerville Chamber of Commerce. April 29, 1999.

NEWSPAPERS

Austin American-Statesman. July 10, 1956.
Brenham Banner Press. July 6-10, 1956.
Houston Post. July 10, 1956.

CHAPTER 19
INTERVIEWS

John J. Klevenhagen Jr. November 24, 1998.

LETTERS

Sheriff John J. Klevenhagen Jr. May 5, 1989. Report on submachine guns confiscated in Galveston raids.

BOOKS

Cartwright, Gary. *Galveston: A History of the Island*. Atheneum. New York. 1991.

SCHOLARLY JOURNAL

Southwestern Historical Quarterly. "Galveston as a Tourist City" by David G. McComb. Texas State Historical Association. January 1997.

NEWSPAPERS

Houston Post. June 11, 14-16, 18, 1957.

CHAPTER 20

INTERVIEWS

John J. Klevenhagen Jr. November 24, 1998.
Carolyn Klevenhagen. November 24, 1998.
Viola Klevenhagen. November 24, 1998.
Edgar Gooding. December 17, 1998.

LETTERS

Homer Garrison Jr. to Texas Ranger Captain John J. Klevenhagen Sr. April 21, 1958.
Name withheld to Texas Ranger E.L. Oliver. November 29, 1958.

LIBRARY ARCHIVES

Vertical file on James Marion West. Center for American History, University of Texas at Austin.
Resolution of the Texas House of Representatives. H.R.S. No. 46. November 1958.

BOOKS

Bainbridge, John. *The Super-Americans*. Doubleday & Company. Garden City, NY. 1961.
Dorman. *King of the Courtroom*.

Fuermann, George. *Houston: Land of the Big Rich*. Doubleday & Company. Garden City, NY. 1951.

McComb, David G. *Houston the Bayou City*. University of Texas Press. Austin. 1969.

McMurty, Larry. *In A Narrow Grave: Essays on Texas*. Encino Press. Austin. 1968.

MAGAZINES

Time Magazine. February 3, 1958.

NEWSPAPERS

Dallas Morning News. December 19, 1957. May 28, October 3, 1958.

Houston Post. November 28-30, December 1-2, 1954. April 4, December 18-19, 1957. November 17, 27, 29, 1958. December 27, 1968.

New York Sunday News. May 17, 1953.

San Antonio Express. November 28-29, 1958. Undated interview with retired Texas Ranger Jerome Preiss.

CHAPTER 21

INTERVIEWS

John J. Klevenhagen Jr. November 24, 1998.
John J. Klevenhagen III. August 28, 1999.
Carolyn Klevenhagen. August 28, 1999.

NEWSPAPERS

Houston Chronicle. October 7, 1962. May 14-18, 1999.

Index

A

Albright, Frank, 31
Allee, Alfred, 152, 157-158

B

Balinese Room, 201-203
Ball, "Alligator" Joe, 35-40
Ball, Dolores, 45
Banks, Jay, 183
Barber, Gene, 196
Beaumont, Texas, 61
Bell, R.J., 29
Biaggne, Frank, 202
Brannan, John, 179
Bridge, Joe, 152
Brown, Caro, 158
Brown, Hazel, 35, 41-43
Brown, Jedidiah, 123-125

C

Carlino, Diego, 88, 93-101
Carver, Duke, 14
Cervantes, Alfredo, 151
Clark, Marvin, 108-109
Cohen, Mickey, 103
Collins, Rip, 17
Comal County, Texas, 1
Connell, Frank, 192
Crosby, Robert James, 161, 165
Cude, Elton, 37
D
Daniel, Price, 156, 203, 207, 220
Doolin, Doyce C., 161

Dukes of Duval, 147-159

E

Ellisor, Archie, 164-171
Ellisor, Merle, 164-171

F

FBI, 79, 225
Flores, Helen, 139
Floyd, Jacob "Jake," 151
Floyd, Jacob "Buddy" Jr., 151
Foreman, Percy, 88-91, 97-103, 210
Fort Travis, 251
Frazier, Lloyd, 65
Freedom Party, 150

G

Galveston, Texas, 199-208
Garrison, Homer, 53-54, 217
Giacona, Sam, 69-72
Gladney, Robert, 220
Gooding, Ed, 204, 207, 215, 217
Gotthardt, "Big" Minnie, 38, 40, 44, 46-49
Gray, John, 35, 40

H

Halson, Alton Golden, 187-197
Hardt, Charlie, 189, 192
Hauck, Bill, 6, 144
Heard, Cyrus, 18
Hightower, Cato, 182, 184-186
Hill, Gladwyn, 147, 157
Houston, Texas, 81-82

Humphrey, Carl, 182
Hutchinson, Donald, 71-72

J

Johnson, Leroy "Pegleg,"
    135-144
Johnson, Lyndon, 148-149
Jung, Arthur Henry, 127-134

K

Keen, Jimmy, 100
Kern, C.V. "Buster," 22, 69,
    86-87, 102, 141, 218-220,
    222
Kilday, Owen, 12
Klevenhagen, Carolyn, 226
Klevenhagen, John J. "Johnny,"
    9, 52, 60, 79, 208, 217
Klevenhagen, John J. Jr., 52,
    105, 119, 121, 122,
    196-197, 219, 223-227
Klevenhagen, John J. III, 226
Klevenhagen, Kara, 226
Klevenhagen, Viola Wolff, 7, 67,
    122, 218, 220, 226

L

Lane, "Buckshot," 176
Lewis, Janice, 191, 195
Lewis, Milton "Romeo,"
    188-192, 196-197
Lucas, Rufe, 75-79
Lyles, James, 121

M

Maceo-Dickinson Line, 84, 201
Maceo, Rose, 200
Maceo, Sam, 85, 200
Martin, Patrick, 29
Mason, W.H. "Bill," 150
McCamey, Joe, 59-60
McCarthy, Glen, 83, 107

McGill, Joe, 124-125
Miers, Bobby, 135-146

N

Nevin, David, 156
New Braunfels, Texas, 1
Niemann, Edmund, 137
Norris, Gene Paul, 173-178,
    183-186
Norris, Pete, 174-176
Northcutt, Harry, 25-34

O

Oliver, Ed, 58, 63, 116, 207

P

Parr, Archie, 148, 157-158
Parr, George, 148, 158-159
Payton, Brad, 17
Payton, Leon, 18
Payton, Norman, 17
Philadelphia Shipworks, 61
Preiss, Jerome, 222
Purvis, Hardy, 55, 63

R

Ramsey Prison Farm, 120
Rea, Lawrence, 13-23, 52
Redding, Stan, 67, 78
Rhodes, Waddell L., 128-130

S

San Antonio, Texas, 5
Sapet, Mario "The Turk," 151,
    158
Scarborough, Jimmy, 162-163
Sears, Cecil, 192-193
Sendemer, Andrew, 138
Shamrock Hotel, 83
Shaw, Raymond, 127-134
Shepperd, John Ben, 148
Shivers, Allan, 146, 156, 203
Shook, Lawrence, 52

Siegal, Bugsy, 103
Smith, H.W., 142
Smith, Zeno, 152-154
Smithwick, Sam, 150
Stevenson, Coke, 148
Sutton, John F., 95-96, 101

T

Thompson, W.R, 142
Thorbus, Richard, 135, 137-138, 144
Turner, James Madison III, 112-118

V

Vallone, Vincent, 84-85

W

Walters, J.D., 69, 71-72
Wells, Selvie Winfield, 25-34
West, James Marion "Silver Dollar Jim," 211-215
Wheeler, Clifton, 41-45, 49
Willard, Lewis, 193-194
Williams, E.B., 103
Wilson, Will, 203
Wood, Will, 7, 37, 51